Managing Your Placement

Managing Your Placement

A skills-based approach

Ian Herbert

and

Andrew Rothwell

First published 2005 by
PALGRAVE MACMILLAN
Houndmills, Basingstoke, Hampshire RG21 6XS and
175 Fifth Avenue, New York, N.Y. 10010
Companies and representative throughout the world

PALGRAVE MACMILLAN is the global academic imprint of the Palgrave
Macmillan division of St. Martin's Press, LLC and of Palgrave Macmillan Ltd.
Macmillan® is a registered trademark in the United States, United Kingdom
and other countries. Palgrave is a registered trademark in the European
Union and other countries.

ISBN 978-0-333-98728-5   ISBN 978-1-137-07051-7 (eBook)

DOI 10.1007/978-1-137-07051-7

This book is printed on paper suitable for recycling and made from fully
managed and sustained forest sources.

A catalogue record for this book is available from the British Library.

A catalog record for this book is available from the Library of Congress.

10   9   8   7   6   5   4   3   2   1
14 13 12 11 10 09 08 07 06 05

To
Patricia, **Tracey**, **Stephen** and **Kendrah**
Frances and **Tom**
Thank you for your support and inspiration

Contents

List of figures and tables

FIGURES

TABLES

Preface

Do you want to get the best possible job on leaving higher education? Then look around at the competition – your fellow students – and decide how *you* are going to make *your* CV stand out in the crowd. How are you going to get on the interview shortlist and then land that plum job out of, say, over 100 applications when everyone else has similar academic qualifications?

The simple answer is to present a convincing case to employers to show that you can do something for them. The difference often comes down to how you present your skills and potential. Past experience of work, education and life in general is your showcase. This is your opportunity to provide clear evidence that you can: work hard; be a member of a team; show initiative; learn faster than the rest; stick at mundane tasks when necessary and generally make a contribution to an organisation.

This book will help you to understand the importance of combining work experience with academic learning and how to make the most of your talents, especially during the placement. It will also help you to plan your early career and convince an employer that you have a clear direction and purpose in life.

Work experience may take many forms, including part-time work during term time or vacations. It also comes with a variety of different terms including: work-integrated learning, co-operative education, sandwich courses, etc. We shall be looking at each option in turn and demystifying the confusing array of terms commonly used by educators and employers.

Throughout we will take a skills-based approach, explaining what skills employers need, and how you might acquire skills and improve your employability through education and work experience.

Getting the best place possible is only one part of the story. Will it be the right placement for you? What do you really want to do in the long term? How will you get the best career opportunity after finishing your degree? These are all important questions and this book will set placement within an overall context that sees your lifelong employability being continually enhanced through a structured framework of skills.

IAN HERBERT
ANDREW ROTHWELL

Acknowledgements

The authors and publishers are grateful to the following for permission to reproduce copyright material:

The Derbyshire Business School for permission to reproduce 'Benefits of employing placement students' and practical examples of placement experience.

Her Majesty's Stationery Office for permission to reproduce Tables 1.1 and 1.2 from the Dearing Report (National Committee for Inquiry into Higher Education).

Prentice Hall for permission to reproduce Figure 3.3, The Kolb learning cycle.

Careers Service, University of Newcastle upon Tyne, for permission to reproduce Figure 1.2, Learning opportunities.

Plain English Campaign for permission to reproduce examples of translation.

NCWE for permission to reproduce list of 'Quality in a placement' on pages 27–8 (www.work-experience.org).

Thanks also go to employers and colleagues who have kindly offered suggestions, and to students whose experiences in finding and undertaking placements have provided valuable insights into learning and working life.

List of Abbreviations

AGCAS	Association of Graduate Careers Advisory Services
AGR	Association of Graduate Recruiters
CPD	Continuing Professional Development
CV	curriculum vitae
HASAW	Health And Safety At Work Act
HE	higher education
HEI	higher education institution
ICT	Information and communication technology
IT	Information Technology
NCVQ	National Council for Vocational Qualifications
NCWE	National Council for Work Experience
PEST	political, economic, social, technology
PINT	framework of transferable skills used in this book
QAA	Quality Assurance Agency
SMART	Specific, measurable, achievable, realistic, time-bound
SMEs	Small and medium-sized enterprises
STEP	Shell Technology Enterprise Programme
SWOT	strengths, weaknesses, opportunities, threats

Please note

The wide variety of study programmes presently available in further and higher education together with an infinitely variable range of work experience options make it difficult in a single book to cover all the options all the time. For simplicity, it is assumed that a 'programme of study' is a four-year undergraduate degree at a university with a year on a placement between the second and third years of study (a sandwich degree). It is stressed that this should not be seen as in any way excluding other institutions or indeed qualifications, such as Higher National Certificates and Diplomas; neither does it exclude periods of work placement shorter than one year.

This book in itself cannot provide detailed coverage of every aspect of starting your career. Instead it is designed to provide an overview of how you might best combine learning with work, and work with learning, during higher education. Signposts throughout the text and on the accompanying web site will suggest further references and sources of help and guidance.

You should always consult your own programme leader or specialist placement/career advisers before making any final decisions.

Part I

Work-related experience and skill development

1

Why do a placement? The importance of work-related learning

By the end of this chapter you will understand:

- the importance of integrating work and study
- what employers are looking for
- what is meant by work-related learning
- the benefits of doing a placement
- the range of placement and part-time work experience available

INTRODUCTION: INTEGRATING WORK AND STUDY

This book is ultimately designed to help students get a better job after graduation. Taking a structured approach to learning from practical work experience combined with academic study will help you to present the best possible case of your competence and potential to an employer.

Job hunting is about getting on the shortlist and then beating the competition. There is seldom any consolation in coming second. We believe that the best way to prepare yourself for a career in your chosen field is to take a holistic view to learning. That means combining academic study with practical work experience and being able to appreciate and demonstrate the linkages between the two. One significant opportunity to gain quality work experience is through an industrial placement within a degree programme.

This book will help in the following ways:

1   For school leavers it will help you to decide, before you go to university or a college of further education, how you might benefit from undertaking a degree programme that includes a period of work experience in industry and what form that might take.

2   Once you have started studying, we will show you how to take stock of your talents and ambitions and then plan your strategy for getting the placement you want. Specific chapters will cover the various stages of making job applications that will capitalise on all your skills and work experience.

3   When out on placement the book will continue to support you in managing and documenting your experience.

Finally, you will benefit from having a framework that will help you to reflect upon your work experiences and document them in a form ready for job hunting after graduation.

However ...

It is not the style of this book to say that you should do a placement or that it would suit everyone. First, careers, work and education are infinitely varied and a 'one shoe fits all' approach is not only inappropriate but could seriously damage your wealth. Second, the direction of your career and the success of the various steps along the way are your responsibility and the whole process needs to be a self-managed one.

The importance of practical experience

Employers are increasingly placing more importance during selection on an applicant's ability to learn through practical experience. Traditionally, employers have selected young people on the basis that they were generally bright and had the right attitude for work. Specialist training and instruction would then equip the trainee to do whatever specific tasks were required in that particular organisation.

However, an increasing number of organisations today expect applicants to be able to tell the selection panel exactly what *they* have to offer now and how *they* will make a contribution. The buzz-phrase is being able to 'hit the ground running': in other words, needing very little time

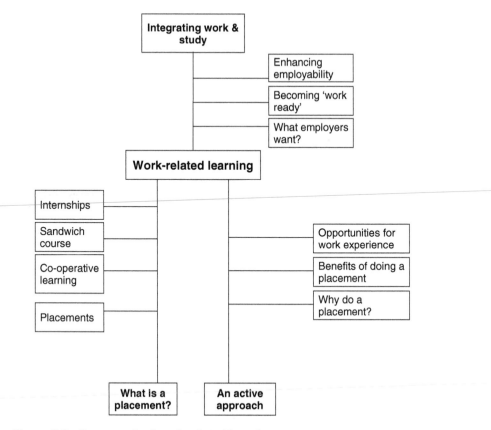

Figure 1.1 Framework of work-related learning

and only minimal training before starting to pay back the salary! However, it's not all bad news.

Opportunities to advance and enjoy real responsibility – together with attractive salaries – in the early years of work tend to be much better than in the past, though this does mean that young people have to take much more responsibility for planning, developing and maintaining their own learning and projecting their competence. In today's world, you need not only to manage your own career but also to be your own public relations agent as well!

We shall encourage you to see work experience as part of a wider learning process which will prepare you for the rest of your life. At the same time we will help you to gather the evidence that will allow you to convince a future employer that *you* are the right person for the job. Figure 1.1 shows how you might think about this process.

WHAT EMPLOYERS EXPECT

Employability

There was a time, up until around the early 1990s, when an academic qualification in itself was usually sufficient to get the first job after leaving education, the first step of a life-long career. Such jobs were usually based on a formal training programme (often a graduate training programme for 2 to 3 years). During this time trainees would spend a period of time in a succession of different departments and functions whilst undertaking training courses and perhaps additional education on a day/block release basis. Meaningful and responsible tasks did not tend to be given or expected until the period of 'apprenticeship' was completed. The term 'employability' is often used to describe long-term potential in employees; it is covered in detail in Chapter 9.

Work-readiness

In the last 10 years or so this has changed dramatically. Nowadays, employers expect to recruit people from higher education who have both the necessary academic qualifications and a wide range of skills and experiences. They now seek people who can bring existing skills and knowledge and be able to adapt quickly to a new environment: quite simply, people who need much less training than was the case previously. Training costs money and delays the time when you pay back the employer by doing something useful; in other words, when you are 'work ready'.

In addition to the phrase 'being able to hit the ground running', employers also talk about the need to show that you can 'bring something to the party' (i.e., have existing skills/knowledge that they might not have).

If this sounds like a poor deal compared with the past, then take comfort from the fact that nowadays you have the opportunity to earn better starting salaries and do more interesting work much faster than was previously the norm. Some of the reasons for this change are discussed below. The purpose in discussing it here is that if employers are no longer going to provide a gentle introduction to the world of work and basic training, then you have to do it yourself.

This means that if you want to beat your competitors (fellow students) to the best career jobs you have to demonstrate both employability for the longer term and work-readiness in the shorter term. You will have to have a clear idea of what work-related learning is; how to acquire quality experience; and how to document and articulate your skills to employers. Although it is not the only option, a period of placement work is a fantastic opportunity to do this.

> **Terminology check**
>
> Work-readiness means being ready for work and contributes to your overall level of employability.

SO WHO SAYS I NEED MORE THAN EXAM CERTIFICATES?

We'll now look in more detail about what skills employers are asking for and why they need people with those skills. This is vitally important to appreciate early in your preparation, as you may need to reconsider your approach to part-time work well before you start applying for placement jobs. Furthermore, when you actually start making applications many application forms can only be completed on-line and you will not have the time to research your answers then. You will also need to show that you understand the employer's position and respond to their questions at interview.

When employers say they want something more than exam certificates it is often difficult for them to say exactly what it is they are looking for. There is a confusing array of terms used to describe some of these attributes. Even within individual departments within the same organisation different people will have different views depending on:

- their own background
- the tasks they are presently doing
- their experience of past employees

The following section looks at three perspectives:

- the views of an eminent former 'captain of industry'
- the findings of the Dearing Report into Higher Education
- evidence from some current job vacancies

Chapter 4 will introduce a framework of skills for placement.

EMPLOYERS' VIEWS

Views from the top

Sir John Harvey-Jones, the famous former industrial leader, gives the following advice to young job seekers:

Employers look for signs of initiative and the ability to self-start, which are essential for any managerial success.

They are also looking primarily for qualities of character, since most employers will take the acquisition of a degree as evidence of a clear mind.

People are looking for judgement, the ability to communicate (which means a listening as well as speaking), humanity and concern, openness of mind, and the ability to concentrate and to work hard for a goal which the individual has to buy into.

Sir John is suggesting here that a degree in specific area of study is only a part of what employers are looking for. Of equal importance is your ability to demonstrate qualities of character and a range of general skills. Two other quotes from interviews with employers are interesting:

Yes, but they [students] do have unrealistic expectations about the rate of career progress and the salary increases which they might secure without first proving their value to the company and the real application of new knowledge and skills to take the business forward.

We need practical engineers with excellent communication skills. Often interpersonal and teamwork skills are in need of improvement.

The Dearing Report on Higher Education

Perhaps the most authoritative reference is the extract below which is taken from the Dearing Report on Higher Education. This report was based upon on an extremely thorough research and consultation exercise with all the stakeholders in higher education in the late 1990s. Its recommendations have had a significant influence in the UK Government's education policy since. The report states:

One consequence of the rising number of graduates entering the labour market, and of an increasingly competitive labour market, is that employers are increasingly scrutinising the quality of graduates. In particular, numerous studies suggest that employers want more from graduates.

In addition, they are looking for a range of technical competences and transferable skills, along with general personal and entrepreneurial attributes in their potential recruits.

However, employers are not homogeneous [all the same], their needs and requirements are different and they often cannot identify exactly what they want from graduates. Indeed, consultations with employers undertaken by the NCIHE (National Committee of Inquiry into Higher Education) suggest that less equal proportions of employers are satisfied and dissatisfied with graduates' skills.

Many of these issues have been encapsulated in debates about 'graduateness' and the employability of graduates.

Basically, what this is means is that there is no single understanding of what improves employability but the basic idea is that an individual should display a sense of 'graduateness' and be able to offer appropriate skills to an employer (in other words, a wider range of skills and attributes than simply the technical skills and knowledge traditionally associated with academic competence).

The Dearing Report goes on to list some graduate skills in order of employer preference; we shall deal with these in further Chapter 3.

Current job adverts

Let's now have a look at some examples of what employers are expecting.

Table 1.1 The skills needed by employers from higher education over the next 10–20 years (ranked by the percentage of employers stating a need)

Rank	Skills/attributes	Employers (%) n = 119
1	Business management skills	34
2	Named specialist skills other than business management (a 'catch-all' term)	29
3	Information technology (can you use it easily?)	27
4	Cognitive skills (thinking)	22
5	Learning to learn (can you learn fast and continue developing yourself?)	21
6	Communication skills	21
7	Interpersonal skills/attributes	19
8	Unspecified high level skills (analysis, synthesis, evaluation)	17
9	Flexibility	17
10	Personal skills/attributes	13
11	Practical/vocational skills/qualifications (experience)	11
12	Foreign languages	10
13	Unspecified 'key' or 'core' skills (transferable skills)	6
14	Numerical skills	5
Not ranked	Other*	35

* Although this list seems quite comprehensive, note how large the 'other' category is. Employers have a very wide range of requirements dependent on their business.

Descriptions in brackets are our explanations of the report's terms.

Activity

Look at the following three extracts from advertisements for placement opportunities from well-known organisations, and then answer the following question. What broad types of skills are they looking for? Name five.

Extract 1: Human Resource Management

We look for individuals with varying degrees and levels of experience. All candidates should possess good communication, influencing, problem-solving and customer service skills plus the ability to adapt to change. Candidates should also have the ability to work well in groups, possess strong leadership and judgement skills and excellent analytical skills.

Extract 2: Technical Computer Technology

This company looks for qualified individuals with the right combination of skills, education, research and experience in the following areas:

- strong technical leadership and decision-making skills
- clear, concise verbal and written communication skills for providing crisp direction toward resolving key issues
- firm team-building skills to facilitate cross-functional team effectiveness

Extract 3: Accountancy

We have found that our successful trainees are:

- intelligent, yet practical, common sense people
- hard working, but able to create a balance between their work and personal life
- interested in owner-managed and fast growing entrepreneurial businesses and enjoy giving practical advice
- able to work well in a team, willing to help and to share knowledge and expertise
- good at developing strong relationships with both clients and colleagues
- able to use their knowledge creatively for the benefit of our clients and our business

Five skills required are:

Web link

Follow up these sample adverts for yourself by looking at some job advertisements. Then talk directly to employers at careers events; ask them specifically what they are looking for. To see the top 100 employers in the UK go to the following site and then choose an employer: http://uktop100.reuters.com. Look at their stated needs for graduates in your field.

Activity

Just to get you thinking about these skills, get a copy of your present curriculum vitae (CV) and write down on the outline below some examples of the different skills that you have already mentioned. By 'mentioned', we mean you have clearly stated an example on your CV, not simply mentioned that you worked at XYZ Ltd for 6 months, leaving other people to guess what skills you might have acquired.

Don't worry if you don't understand all the terms or don't have them evidenced on your CV yet; that's precisely where this book is going to help you. By understanding what employers want from you and how you can best present yourself to them you will be able to prepare a much better CV that closely fits what employers are wanting. For examples, see the end of this chapter.

Skills/attributes	Examples
Business management skills	
Named specialist skills (a 'catch-all' term)	
Information technology (can you use it easily?)	
Cognitive skills (thinking)	
Learning to learn (can you learn fast and continue developing yourself?)	
Communication skills	
Interpersonal skills/attributes	
Unspecified high level skills (analysis, synthesis, evaluation)	
Flexibility	
Personal skills/attributes	
Practical/vocational skills/qualifications (experience)	
Foreign languages	
Unspecified 'key' or 'core' skills (transferable skills)	
Numerical skills	
Other	

A copy of this form is on the supporting web site where you can expand the space available between the lines and/or type in your answers if you wish. A sample response for a computing undergraduate can be seen in Appendix 7.

Activity debrief

You may have found this exercise quite hard, in terms both of understanding the terms involved and in realising how few of these skills are explicit on your CV. Don't worry, we will be guiding you through the process of analysing your experience and making the best of your experience in the coming chapters. Next we'll look at how to get good experience to start with.

EMPLOYABILITY: ACTIVE MANAGEMENT OF YOUR DESTINY

If by now you're convinced that you need to be able to offer something more than just an academic qualification, then exactly what do you need for your chosen career path? How do you get it and how will anyone know you have got it?

Well, work experience is a key part of acquiring those qualities and that's what this book is about. Of course, another place to go for advice is the pub. Inevitably there is always at least one person who will say something like, 'I'm doing great. This was the only job I applied for. They didn't ask me about work experience, they could see what I was capable of. All you need is a bit of confidence, the gift of the gab. You make your own luck!'

Well, maybe it can work out that way, but do you want to rely on this approach? What happens if the business goes bust? Then the only bankable thing is your CV! Today, having a 'job-for-life' means having the skills and experience to be sufficiently employable to ensure that someone, somewhere, keeps paying you until you retire.

The nature of work and relationships between employers and employees is undergoing rapid change at present and all the indications are that the pace of change will get faster rather than slower. In the next two sections we will look briefly at how the placement system developed, what you can expect today and how you should view work-related learning as important both now and for your future.

WORK-RELATED LEARNING: A CONTINUAL PROCESS

In this book 'work-related learning' means:

The active acquisition of a range of quality skills and experiences from paid or unpaid employment that will complement a programme of academic study so as to increase the student's sense of work-readiness and long-term employability.

To expand on this definition we mean the following:

1   Work experience that is part of an overall learning process in which work experience helps you to make sense of your theoretical studies at university and conversely to make sense of the work place as a result of studying the theoretical aspects of your target discipline.
2   A range of appropriate skills and competences can be evidenced to underpin job applications upon graduation.
3   Reflection is made upon experience gained and plans for improvements are made within a process of continual learning.
4   Employability is the capability to move self-sufficiently within the labour market to realise potential through sustainable employment (Hillage and Pollard, 1998).
5   Work readiness is the ability to quickly adapt to a new employment situation. This should not mean being able to do any job immediately but an employer would expect that you will be familiar with the work environment and be able to work with minimum supervision once task-specific training/instruction has been given.

WHAT IS WORK EXPERIENCE?

Work experience is any activity outside or within an educational programme that involves working on a paid or unpaid basis for an employer. This may be as a full-time employee on an industrial placement, part-time work during the vacation or term time, or work for a voluntary organisation where the relationship between the individuals and that organisation has been formalised to some extent.

With regard to voluntary organisations there is a fine dividing line between any involvement which is a hobby/interest and a commitment to undertake specific tasks or duties on a regular basis which might otherwise be paid but for which you happen to give your time freely. For example, an employer will probably view a six-week stint working within, say, a charity shop as work experience, whereas being the treasurer for the local football team is more likely to be seen as an interest associated with a hobby.

However, there is no such thing as worthless work experience: even the most mundane jobs can be a learning experience and useful evidence of your ability to apply yourself to a task, to work as a team, to operate in a disciplined manner, to follow instructions, etc. We shall look at this aspect in more detail in Chapter 3.

There is a range of opportunities that will help you to experience working situations; see Figure 1.2.

OPPORTUNITIES FOR WORK-RELATED LEARNING

It is difficult to say what is good or not so good experience. No work experience is likely to be viewed negatively unless it is illegal or verging on the immoral! However, being serious, you have to consider the learning and development opportunities within your own portfolio. For example, being a deck chair attendant on a beach in the South of France for the summer holidays might provide evidence in respect of:

- language skills
- dealing with customers
- handling cash, having responsibility
- application
- willingness to travel and find work overseas, etc.

However, doing this every year or for a whole year will not add much to your skill base and will soon be seen as displaying little initiative.

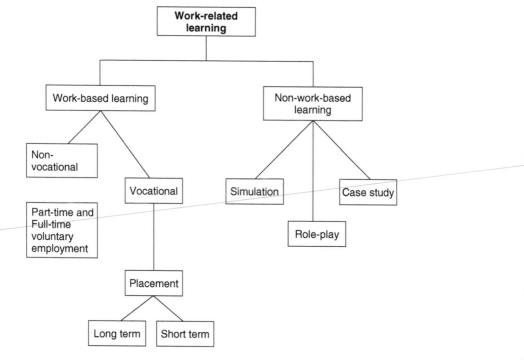

Figure 1.2 Learning opportunities

Source: Allison, J., Freeman, P. and Nixon, I. (2001).

WHAT IS A PLACEMENT?

Placements now take many different forms and the term itself can be somewhat misleading. A quick search of the Internet will result in many uses of the term. The majority is employment-related but, nevertheless, does not refer to student opportunities. In terms of what is commonly meant by a student placement, in this book we mean a substantive period of full-time employment in what would otherwise be study time.

Why, though, is such a seemingly odd term used? To answer that it is best to go back in time a little to the start of placements as we know them. Originally, students in the sciences would enjoy a period of time within their courses employed within laboratories or working with practitioners in the field. Specific practical experience was often a requirement of the degree. The total number of students involved was relatively small and university tutors would 'place' their students in suitable positions, often in groups, with the organisations from year to year.

The majority of degree programmes were viewed as essentially academic and a part of a general process of education and development, rather than as preparation for any particular style of vocation. Indeed, some courses still lean towards this. Experience of work on placement was generally well structured, with a predetermined rotation through various departments and tasks, but on the whole the tasks themselves were often low level and more often involved being an observer rather than being responsible for an outcome. Pay also tended to be poor, but was better than grant levels.

Nowadays, it is very much more difficult to say what constitutes a placement and in the context of this book the term can be misleading. Whilst many institutions facilitate the contact of students and employers, to a greater or lesser extent most take the view that it is the student's own responsibility to locate and secure employment, as it provides good experience for after university.

We would prefer to use the term 'work-integrated learning' as it more clearly signifies that academic and practical studies should be seen as interdependent. However, students and employers in the UK tend to use the term 'placement' and so we will use that in this book when referring to a programme with a formal period of work-related learning. Alternative terms include the following:

1 *Internships*: this tends to be used in the USA and should be used if approaching employers there.
2 *Sandwich course*: this tends to be used to describe a degree programme (or other qualification) which includes a period of work experience (out on placement).
3 *Co-operative education*: this tends to be used to describe partnerships between the organisations in industry and educational institutions, particularly in Europe. The partnerships tend to be long-term with a structured programme combining learning and work experience. See www.waceinc.org.

BENEFITS OF DOING A PLACEMENT

The placement year provides a number of opportunities for students to gain practical experience and thus improve their employment prospects after graduation. Specifically, the benefits of commercial placements can be summarised as follows:

1 Application of subject knowledge gained in the first two years of study.
2 Acquisition of practical experience to underpin case study work and scenario analysis in the final year of study.
3 Development of a range of transferable skills (see Chapter 4).

4 Enhancement of employment prospects by practising job-hunting skills and by building a track record of achievement that will enhance the your CV/reference base.
5 Opportunity to try out possible job types or industry sectors before making long-term career decisions.
6 Development of contacts in industry.
7 Some large employers view the placement year as an extended interview. This can lead to a job on graduation or maybe to part-time work in the final year of study, and occasionally even a sponsor for study.
8 Identification of possible projects for the dissertation/project topics/themes in the final year.
9 Development of character and maturity.
10 *The chance to earn some money!*

Here are some quotes which may help you to make up your mind about the value of doing a placement.

Employers

The box contains two press releases from 2002 and 2003 issued by the Association of Graduate Recruiters (AGR), a body that represents most of the major employers of students. Essentially, they are saying that at graduate level salaries are up but the total number of positions is down in both years. The best jobs are going to the applicants with the right skills. Times are indeed getting tougher but more interesting! They also touch briefly on placements in 2003, although this is not the AGR's main focus.

Graduate vacancies drop – skills are key to success

Graduate employers are predicting a drop in vacancies this year, but salaries are on the way up, and graduates with the right skills can demand healthy packages.

(AGR, 18 February 2002)

Employers report a slight fall in graduate level vacancies

This year's graduates are facing a tighter job market, according to figures released today by AGR.

A survey of some of the UK's leading employers is reporting a 3.4 per cent drop in UK graduate level vacancies this year compared with the numbers of graduates recruited in 2002, reflecting the

---

current cautious economic climate. Along with this fall in vacancies, the survey also indicates increased competition for graduate jobs in the UK. Employers received an average of 42.1 applications for every graduate vacancy during the 2002–3 recruitment year compared with 37.2 applications per vacancy in 2001–2.

But the median graduate starting salary has climbed to £20,300, an above-inflation rise of 4.3 per cent on 2002. The outlook for 2004 suggests that both salaries and vacancies will remain fairly stable next year.

Work experience

The AGR survey indicates that work experience placements remain popular with employers. Nearly three quarters (73 per cent) of employers surveyed are offering some form of work placements for undergraduates in 2003–4 and more than half (52 per cent) are offering work experience placements for undergraduates during the 2003 summer holidays.

(AGR, 16 July 2003)

Comments from line managers

On selecting graduates, these included the following.

I think what I notice is that the people who are particularly strong and make a big contribution as a graduate, are those who have done some form of placement year so they have got the combination of practical experience and the theory.

The company places a significant weighting on previous work experience particularly if a placement has been taken within the company or alternatively within any finance function. This demonstrates that the candidates know what this type of work is all about and still wants to do it.

We prefer our previous placement students as we've already put quite a bit of investment into their training whilst on placement – presently 50% of them return after graduation.

The final comment is from a manager in the UK office of a large American company talking about what they look for when selecting students for placement.

I think there its [sic] very much people that show ability for thought, commitment, people who can go out and actually know what they want to do and go out and achieve as well. So people that have taken gap years and done something constructive with it would obviously attract us to them rather than somebody who has done nothing.

Quotes from university tutors

The placement makes a tremendous difference: kids go out, adults come back!

The placement marks the crossover in their education from being taught to learning.

Students

The first quotation is from a graduate with one year's post-university experience and the rest are from final-year students, all in response to the question: to what extent did the inclusion of a placement year on your programme help you?

When I first started at XYZ, I was totally amazed at the commercial side of it and how everything needed to be like that, as you were saying earlier. And I really struggled for the first couple of months. It's very different. If you haven't done a work placement in a business and you've just gone straight into audit, I don't think you realise what it's all about.

I think it had a huge effect on both to be honest. I'm a huge fan of the placement year idea. I think it helps add a practical dimension to all the theory that you learn, and I think you also come back more of a rounded – it sounds like a cliché – but more of a rounded individual. You know what you've got to do; you learn to manage time better and things like that.

The placement was very useful with both knowledge and skills being enhanced during the period. It was good to put academic theory into practice and see how it worked in real life. It was also interesting to see some theory that did not really work in practice.

Working in an actual work environment is a fantastic experience and knowledge is quickly built up. Working also allows you to develop as a person and become more confident in things like presentations. The experience gained was used for nearly all my coursework assignments [in the final year].

A bit of balance

These are obviously very positive views but in the authors' experience the overwhelming majority of students who do placements find them helpful. In fact, it can be depressing as a lecturer when you meet past students and ask them what they liked most about their degree. Usually they say 'the placement': the year they weren't at university!

However, not all degree courses have mandatory placements and where placements are optional it tends to be that students opt to finish their degree sooner rather than later. Placements are just one option in your overall employability. Our advice is that you need to be thinking about the possibility of placement *before you choose your degree programme* by finding out what the employers' views are in your specialist field and deciding whether it is right for you.

Appendix 2 provides a series of questions that you might ask admission tutors when considering which degree programme and which university to apply to.

SUMMARY

You should now appreciate the need to demonstrate a range of skills to an employer evidenced by quality work experience in conjunction with formal education. The next chapter will look in more detail at work experience in more depth and placement opportunities.

References

Allison, J., Freeman, P. and Nixon, I. (2001) *ASET Annual Conference Proceedings (2001)*, Association for Sandwich Education Training.

Harvey-Jones, J. (n.d.) *Prospects' 94, Guide to Graduate Opportunities*, PXP: The Careers Service.

Hillage, J. and Pollard, E. (1998) *Employability: Developing a Framework for Policy Analysis*, DFEE Publications.

Further reading

Handy, C.B. (1995) *The Empty Raincoat*, PXP: Random House Business Books.

If you like Handy's style of writing then try this follow-up book: *Beyond Certainty: The Changing Worlds of Organisations* (1995) London: Random House. This is a collection of essays on work and organizational life in which the author shares his reflections on a changing world.

Also, try a lively read from the best-selling American author and management guru, Tom Peters: *The Pursuit of Wow!* (1995) London: Macmillan. It covers wide-ranging topics such as people's love of 'bigness', building the curious corporation, how crisis can be a teacher and what to do when failure looks like success.

Also worth a look on organisation and behaviour theory are: Greenberg, J. and Baron, R.A. (2002), *Behaviour in Organizations*, 6th edn, New York: Prentice Hall and Mintzberg, H. (1998), *Structuring of Organizations*, PXP London: Prentice Hall.

2

Learning through work: the changing nature of work and employment markets

May you live in interesting times.

Chinese proverb

By the end of this chapter you will understand:

- how organisations are changing
- what this means for job hunting
- what is meant by good quality work experience
- what types of placement opportunity are available

INTRODUCTION

In the last chapter we looked at what employers were expecting to see in job applications. Unfortunately, the world of work is changing fast and it would be foolish not to also try to understand why and how organisations are changing and look briefly at the effect on recruitment and selection processes.

WHAT IS CHANGING?

Again we find that individual organisations seem to be experiencing different patterns of change in their environment. To see some of the

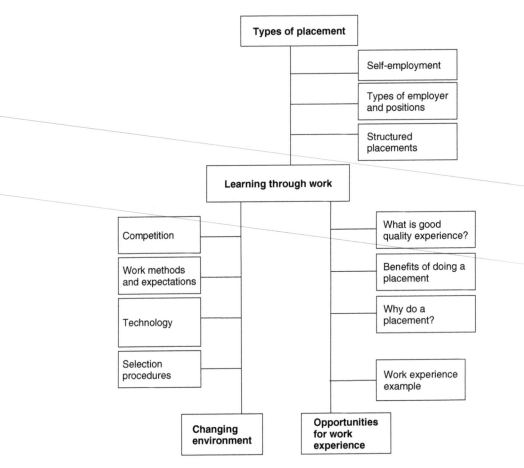

Figure 2.1   Learning through work: context and opportunities

major impacts as ranked by employers we will return to the Dearing Report. Table 2.1 shows issues ranked in order of importance.

> [These changes] may well mean that the company will require fewer graduates, etc. – particularly engineers – as activities are outsourced to external providers. Clearly the need for these skills will be as great as ever before, but this need will have been transferred to supplier companies. (Dearing Report (1996), evidence from survey of employers)

WHY ARE THINGS CHANGING?

Let's have a more detailed look at what is driving some of these factors.

Table 2.1   The main factors likely to determine an employer's workforce and patterns of working over the next 10 to 20 years

Rank	Main factor	Employers (%) n = 119
1	Technology	49
2	Customers/clients market	44
3	Labour: employee wants/labour market	40
4	Flexibility	29
5	Labour: outsourcing	23
6	Labour: skills	23
7	International/globalisation	17
8	Costs and quality of graduates	5
Not ranked	Other	50

Greater competitive pressures

Globalisation, the process of removing impediments to trade between countries, has created greater competitive pressure for firms which compete in overseas markets or supply customers that can buy alternative goods or services from overseas suppliers.

The savings that these pressures have made in terms of cheaper commercial products has not gone unnoticed by public sector organisations and governments who expect year-on-year efficiencies from their own services. Industry now operates on a much shorter timescale. The pace of every aspect of business life is much faster. This speeding-up of life has extended from the private sector of the economy into the public sector.

Greater pressures from investors and stakeholders

In the private sector stock market investors expect better returns on their investments and much more information on how companies are being run. Many managers are under continual pressure to meet annual budgets and short-term performance targets. Again, governments driven by the demands of voters for more efficient public services expect greater output with fewer resources.

Better Information and Communication Technology (ICT)

Major advances in computer equipment and operating programmes continue to improve the efficiency of working methods. This leads to new opportunities for working and collaborating in different ways that were not generally thought of even 10 years ago. Examples of things we now take for granted include: 'business-to-business electronic commerce'; ordering supplies over the Internet electronically; speech recognition programmes, and so on.

Changes in work methods and organisation

Great advances have also been made in understanding how people can better work together and how large organisations can be better organised and managed. You may have heard the terms 'delayering' and 'empowerment'. The first reflects the process of restructuring by taking layers of management out of the organisation chart, as shown below.

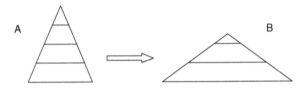

In structure B the same number of people are employed but there are fewer layers of management. The significance of this is that more people are doing rather than supervising, but those doers need to be capable of supervising themselves!

The second is much less easy to define but tries to capture the culture of giving more responsibility to workers who have greater discretion to manage how they do the job. This usually involves working in self-directed work teams with performance being driven by target outputs rather than the traditional style of being told exactly how to do the job with constant supervision to ensure that you do it. The significance of this will be clearer as we discuss the skills that employers expect workers to have.

Different attitudes and expectations of workers

Another factor in this increasing pace of life is that employees themselves are changing jobs more often than ever before. In the past workers looked to their employers for a lifetime of continued employment. Today, a firm needs to constantly change the shape and make-up of its workforce in response to rapidly changing market conditions. This means that the concept of the so-called 'portfolio worker' is very much the norm. The term was first coined by Charles Handy (1990) and describes a person who takes responsibility for the proactive management of his own career, seeking opportunities and developing skills that will prepare him for the next stage of his own career, rather than leaving his development to the preferences of any one employer. This is also synonymous with the idea of life-long learning for work.

These changes are all a part of a move towards what is called 'the flexible firm', where only a portion of the total people involved still fall into the primary core group of workers. Everyone is a semi-permanent to a greater or lesser degree.

DOES THIS MEAN THE COMPETITION FOR JOBS IS GETTING TOUGHER?

Well the answer is both yes and no. The changes have resulted in a relative period of prosperity and growth from about 1995 and unemployment in 2003 was at a historically low level. However, many more students have been staying on in higher education after the expansion of the early 1990s, and today there is consequently much greater competition for the best jobs. A degree is often now expected rather than special and the following factors mean that competition can be keener for placement and graduation jobs:

1 The effect of lower loyalty to individual employers puts pressure on employers to achieve payback after the initial costs of hiring and training.
2 As a result of government policy towards grants, particularly with tuition fees in England and Wales, together with the rising costs of student accommodation, the vast majority of students now have to undertake part-time and vacation work to support themselves whilst studying. Thus your competitors (fellow students) will have experience of the world of work (fitting in, following instructions, etc.) and some transferable work skills.
3 A further consequence of the funding issue is that many students are finding it difficult to justify the traditional character-building gap year, and quite rightly want to graduate and start earning as fast as possible. Sadly, this can also leave a 'gap' in life skills on the CV.
4 The advent of home/school computing means that good information technology (IT) skills can now be expected by employers, whereas IT used to be viewed as purely a business thing and employers had to provide the training if they wanted you to use it.

To get on the shortlist for interview you need to demonstrate and provide real evidence of your abilities and what value you can add. On the plus side, the rapid changes also provide an opportunity for those students who better prepare themselves for the new conditions to shine. As Charles Darwin famously stated: 'It is not the strongest or the most intelligent species that survives but the ones that can adapt fastest to new conditions.'

WHAT DOES THIS MEAN FOR JOB HUNTING?

When applying

The market is more competitive and you have to have a better, more targeted and focused, CV to get on the shortlist.

To get the job at interview you have to demonstrate clearly that you can do something for the employer to justify the salary, and be able to offer them more in the long term than other applicants.

You have to prove that you can contribute to their mission and as there will be other people with similar qualifications the only way you can achieve what you want is to:

- get a range quality work/life experience
- evidence it on your CV
- align it to the job description
- demonstrate your skills at interview

and do those all those things better than the rest!

Note that good quality, life-enriching experiences (hobbies, sport and involvement with societies) should not be discounted, but they need to be balanced with work experience and made relevant to the job/career you are seeking.

Doing the job

Many employers are now recruiting later in the annual cycle (following the academic year finishing around June/July). In the past the so-called 'milk-round' (employers going to the top universities looking for the best talent or 'cream') tended to be in the autumn for a start in the following summer/autumn. Nowadays, whilst some large employers still have closing dates in October, November and December, many placement jobs do not get advertised until the spring and even as late as the early summer.

Many placement jobs are tending to become 'doing' rather than 'training' jobs: in other words, being appointed to an actual role with specific responsibilities, rather than following a training programme moving from department to department where the emphasis is on experiencing rather than responsibility.

Very short-term appointments might be offered and two six-month placements might give a wider range of experience, although there is obviously the risk of not getting another high-quality placement when the first job comes to an end.

WHAT IS 'GOOD QUALITY' WORK EXPERIENCE?

There is perhaps no such thing as 'bad' quality work experience as you can learn something from all experiences in life. However, we think it important that you seek to build a 'portfolio'* of different but complementary experiences that demonstrate progression in your competence to an employer. The actual experience could take the form of short-term or longer-term full-time or part-time employment; it could be paid or unpaid. It could be work before the placement or the placement itself. Your objective should be to look for new learning opportunities and get them evidenced wherever possible.

*Portfolio is a common term in some careers where physical evidence of past work is appropriate such as in the arts or creative advertising; however, it is now also being used in other spheres to mean a range of experiences.

Quality in a placement

In terms of the placement itself it is suggested that the following aspects should be present in a good quality work experience (adapted with the permission of NCWE: www.work-experience.org.

- the student is guided by the higher education institution (HEI) to identify potential learning outcomes
- objectives are set (by HEI, employer and student)
- supervision is by a supervisor trained in the objectives and learning outcomes of work experience, and academic supervision and visit(s) take place
- regular feedback is given
- an appraisal is given during the work experience and at the end
- where appropriate, a project is undertaken
- learning and achievements are articulated by the student in written form

- an assessment is made, including an assessment of development of skills (by HEI, employer and student)
- recognition, credit or a certificate is awarded

The code of best practice in graduate recruitment sets out a series of responsibilities for students, employers and areas advisory services. Whilst this code does not specifically mention placement of undergraduates we would suggest that the guidelines are equally applicable to placement recruitment and employment.

Quality in part-time work

These ideals will not be possible for all work experience, for example, part-time bar work. However, as a guide we would recommend the following aspects be considered as good practice in terms of learning quality:

- the work has some variety of tasks, responsibilities and objectives
- feedback is given by the employer (team leader/supervisor)
- appraisal is undertaken at the end of the experience
- learning and achievements are articulated by the student in written form
- an assessment is made of skills development (by student) with employer endorsement

Let's now have a look at an example of typical student work.

Activity

Think about the following questions, which are typical of those common at interviews:

1   What work experience do you have?
2   Tell us more about your summer job at XYZ Ltd.
3   What things did you find difficult?
4   How did you learn how to solve those issues/get better?

Pick one of your part-time jobs and use your experience to answer those questions as if at interview.

Debrief

Whilst such questions can be hard enough to answer in the heat of an interview the employer is essentially looking for the following things:

- you are capable of learning and development
- you have acquired skills that are relevant to the position applied for
- you are capable of giving a succinct and informative account of something

We shall deal with the first issue in detail in Chapter 4 but for now we shall look at how to respond an employer in two distinct stages; first, by giving a short factual account of your role and duties and then reflecting upon it as a learning and development experience.

Example of work experience

Last summer I worked in the warehouse of a department store for 6 weeks, working on average 30 hours a week. My duties included:

- receiving requisitions from shop floor departments and locating the goods.
- putting the correct goods into trolleys that would be taken up to the shop floor after closing time.
- entering completed issues and returns on to the computer.
- dealing with emergency requests during shop hours.
- unloading lorries.

Commentary

This is a short factual account of the role and specific duties. It would be sufficient for listing within the past employment section of your CV or for an initial response at interview. However, it does not give an employer any real sense of how you actually did the job, what level of responsibility was involved or what you might have learnt from the experience. You will need to think carefully about what else the job entailed and perhaps incorporate this in your CV in a brief commentary on your skills or use it to illustrate responses to further questions at interview.

Let's now have a look at this second stage for this hypothetical student.

Main challenges

It was hard work both mentally and physically; most people had been there for years and could work very quickly, but I soon got used to it.

It was difficult to understand the stock coding system as some departments did not use item descriptions and there were over 20,000 different items in stock. The supervisor who was meant to be instructing me went off sick in my first week.

How I coped

To cope with the complexity of the coding system I asked another supervisor for the overall coding system document that explained how the system worked and the logic behind the codes. For example, most items were coded by department (e.g., perfumes, carpets etc.) but some things like 'electrical white goods, EL' could be sold by several departments which was confusing. I then followed some examples of the coding structure around the shop floor physically. It then made a lot more sense. After about a week I was making far fewer mistakes.

What else did I learn?

I also learnt more about how to handle people who were getting irate.

Example

Often customers would give a lot of grief to shop floor staff about delays in getting goods they had ordered and the staff would sometimes take out the customer's frustrations on the warehouse staff when usually it wasn't our fault.

Usually, we could sympathise with the shop floor staff – it wasn't their fault either – but often it could seem almost personal. I dealt with such instances by staying calm and making a real effort to get all the facts right about who had ordered what and when and what the computer records were actually showing.

It helped to talk about things in the third person, for example as 'the system' or 'orders being placed' rather than getting personal by saying things like 'you' and 'your department' did this, that, or the other. If things became really difficult I would tell them I would look into it and ask the supervisor.

Final analysis

There are a lot of key skills being evidenced here in a very simple example of a brief, and somewhat mundane, summer job. Issues that an employer is likely to identify include the following.

1 Clear explanation of duties and timescale.
2 Can cope with hard work and not embarrassed about doing mundane work.
3 Is prepared to seek help in learning.
4 Can figure out the appropriate approach to learning in a given situation (demonstrates a structured way to acquiring knowledge).
5 Can see beyond immediate situation and can empathise with others.
6 Can analyse and evaluate a situation: again, not afraid to ask for help/advice.
7 Has demonstrated a good example of interpersonal skills (dealing with instructions and queries, handling complaints).
8 Put experiences in a positive and mature manner rather than 'rubbishing' the other company.

Note that there needs to be some thought as to how to get your points across to an employer. Some information will need to be in your CV to 'whet the appetite' and get as far as the interview shortlist; the rest will need to come out at interview, and later chapters will help you to plan your overall approach.

The remainder of this chapter will look at how you can identify and accumulate a range of good quality work experience.

Activity

Describe some of the specific challenges that you might have faced in undertaking your duties in the job you described earlier and use the example above to illustrate how you approached them in a positive manner and what the outcomes were.

OPPORTUNITIES TO COMBINE WORK AND STUDY

Figure 2.2 represents some of the learning opportunities available in your journey from secondary school to a first career appointment after graduation. The section following concentrates on the form that work experience *within* the degree programme might take.

Traditional one-year placement

The traditional model for placements tends to be structured around a period of nine to twelve months of work for a single employer.

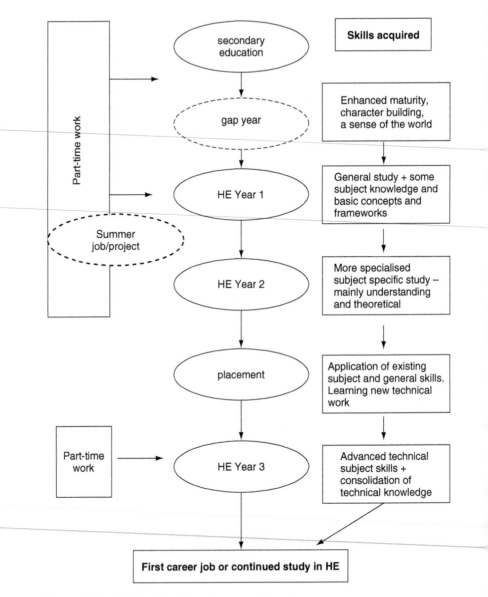

Figure 2.2   Work-related learning a continual process

Sometimes the university placement manager may appoint or 'place' students with particular employers. This is how the idea of industrial placements first started and why we tend to use this term in the UK. It is still the preferred form in some universities, especially in the physical sciences.

Individual employers tend to take a similar number of students from a given university from year to year. The advantages of this is that students do not have to worry about how to find and negotiate a placement themselves, saving what can be a considerable amount of time applying for vacancies. The disadvantages are: first, there is no personal experience of the job-hunting process and, second, the appointment to an individual company is often at the discretion of the placement officer and may not be right for the individual.

The alternative model is where placement managers encourage students to seek and apply for their own placements, whilst also encouraging employers to advertise the placement positions through the university. This gives students a much wider range of options, together with invaluable experience of job-hunting. However, job hunting can be a very time-consuming and challenging job in itself, particularly when time is required for second-year studies.

Making applications to companies that have not had placement students before may also involve the need to explain to those companies what a placement is all about and make sure that sufficient learning and development opportunities are included within the work. See Appendices 3 and 4 for typical roles and tasks on placement.

Working overseas

A placement overseas offers the chance to experience different types of work and social cultures. It is also likely to impress future employers, especially those with a global outlook. It will help you to demonstrate that you also have an international outlook and the drive and determination to do something about it. In addition, you will have the chance to put language skills into practice.

There is a great deal of specialist help available to help you to research overseas opportunities. It helps to try and narrow down your interest to one or two specific types of work or countries as soon as possible, otherwise the potential choice can seem overwhelming and confusing.

There are a number of schemes set up to facilitate the exchange of students between countries. However, these schemes don't always live up to expectations since traditionally there are relatively few UK students who are prepared to enter into reciprocal visits compared with the number of overseas students wishing to come to the UK. This puts placement managers in somewhat tricky positions as regards arranging future visits. However, don't be afraid to ask the question as many students do go abroad and generally gain much from the experience.

Popular destinations for the UK students tend to be the English-speaking countries such as America, Australia and Canada (or at least the

English-speaking part of Canada). The European mainland seems to be much less popular except with students studying European languages and this is a pity.

Many students are attracted by the idea of work experience in the USA (internships) although there is a need to get a US work permit and there may be restrictions. It is usually not problematic to arrange the necessary documentation (visas, work permits), health cover, etc. through one of the specialist US internship programmes. See Chapter 10 for organisations offering programmes international placements aimed at UK students.

Project or short-term work

A growing number of students are finding that their year out on placement is made up of two or even more short-term positions on projects. Such opportunities can be rewarding but obviously there is a risk of maintaining continuous employment. A particularly attractive way of widening your experience is the Shell STEP programme, (see www.step.org.uk). It is often possible to negotiate a later starting date with an employer to allow participation in such schemes. Students should be wary, however, of working for temporary employment agencies as the scope of this work can be somewhat limiting, particularly if the student has little prior work experience.

Worth a look

The Shell Technology Enterprise Programme (STEP) places over 1,500 students a year

The Shell Technology Enterprise Programme (STEP) gives undergraduates the opportunity to gain valuable work experience during the summer holidays and places over 1,500 students a year with small and medium sized businesses. Since it began in 1986, STEP has grown into a well-established national programme, which also enables students to work specifically on environmental projects through 'STEP into the Environment', and in voluntary organisations through 'STEP into the Community'. In 1999, STEP Enterprises Limited was launched in order to build on the success of STEP and to develop the programme further. The company will be supported initially by Shell and other corporate sponsors, but will ultimately become self-supporting.

Source: www.step.org.uk.

Voluntary work

There are a number of extremely good opportunities to gain valuable work experience, particularly overseas, working in voluntary organisations. Not surprisingly with the advent of tuition fees and other financial pressures of student life, fewer students are opting to undertake a placement year on a voluntary basis. However, if there is a particular sphere of work that you might eventually wish to pursue then you could well benefit from a stint with a voluntary organisation. There may even be grants available to support you. Evidence of voluntary work on your CV can demonstrate that you don't simply do things for the money and the range of interpersonal skills developed can be significant. See Chapter 10 where there is a section on volunteering, and in particular the 'crazy paving approach'.

'Placements' after graduation

It may sound rather odd doing a placement after you've graduated but this can be a viable option if you were on a degree programme that didn't include the opportunity to do a placement and you do not yet feel sure about your eventual career direction. Perhaps you are thinking about a further spell in higher education, such as a master's degree. Whilst just getting a full-salary job might seem the obvious, and indeed pressing, choice, there may well be advantages in a placement-style job:

1 There is no commitment beyond the period of the contract.
2 Whilst the salary will usually be a good deal lower than a permanent position, you will probably have more opportunities to move between departments in an organisation and thus get wider experience whilst still earning a living.
3 Placement jobs tend to be less demanding than regular jobs and this will give you the opportunity for part-time study.

If you are on the point of graduation but still feel that a placement-style vacancy might be appropriate, then talk to the placement officers in your university. See if any of the placement employers are prepared to offer you a position that will give you a broader experience of work than you might otherwise get. It may be that you can combine a job for one year after graduation with some further academic research or study. It may be particularly suitable in between a first degree and a master's degree or when a complete career change is being contemplated.

Taking a year out

Perhaps not for the faint-hearted but something we feel we should mention. If your degree programme doesn't include a formal period of placement you might, with approval of your programme tutors, take the opportunity to delay your studies for year whilst working: such a break in study is sometimes called a period of *intercalation* or *leave of absence*. There is increasing flexibility in the university system, particularly on highly modularised programmes, and it may be an option worth considering. The downside is that when you come back you will have to make new friends again (or it may be that you see this as an opportunity to make two lots of friends during your time at university!). Beware, though: changing years might mean that the regulations governing your degree programme could change slightly and this may or may not be advantageous. If you're thinking of taking this option then talk to your tutor as soon as possible.

Since the advent of tuition fees, some students are seeing intercalation as an opportunity to do a placement whilst avoiding payment of tuition fees. Beware! Your university will not supervise your placement and you will not get the benefit of any separate diploma or certificate of work experience. It may also mean that it is difficult to resolve any problems at work, especially if your employers don't keep their promises to give you good experience and to take an interest in your training. Furthermore, as you are no longer a student this may affect such things as exemption from council tax (in the UK), or your status for discounts such as rail-cards, etc.

Self-employment

Students often ask placement managers if they can start their own businesses during their placement year. Traditionally, self-employment has not been seen as appropriate experience and you might well encounter raised eyebrows to say the least. Indeed, it is very difficult to acquire many of the skills that come through interacting with other people in an organisational environment. It is also more difficult for tutors to monitor your progress and to be sure of your skills acquisition. Other issues such as health and safety at work and employers' liability insurance will also need to be addressed.

However, having stated some of the downsides there are, nevertheless, many skills and experiences that can be gained by breaking out on your own, and we have seen one or two very successful placements on a self-employment basis. It is an option that can bring benefits although, again, it is not for the fainthearted.

Self-employment to most people is unfulfilled dream. Most people contemplate it at some stage during their life but it can be difficult to make the break from the 'fur-lined salary trap' as your career progresses. As mentioned in the introduction, the placement year brings opportunities to do things that you might not readily get the chance to do otherwise.

The authors have supervised a small number of students who have become their own boss with varying degrees of success. In each case it was the right thing to do for them as individuals and those particular students tended to get more out of the placement experience than they might have done working for a large organisation.

Whatever, the venture, the business idea itself needs to be sound, although it doesn't have to be a runaway commercial success. As long as you have enough money to survive personally and don't get into debt then it is the experience that counts!

Generally, our advice would be to get some experience of organisational life, if only because if you are self-employed you will at some stage need to understand how organisations, and the people in them, work and think if you're going to deal successfully with them.

If after thinking about these pros and cons you still want to try a project or set up a business on a self-employed basis (maybe with other students) then see your placement officer and talk it through with them as soon as possible. See also the Shell LiveWire programme below. Chapter 10 shows the experience of one student who set up his own web site selling fashion clothes. Admittedly, this was done during the Internet boom but there are always opportunities for good ideas.

Shell LiveWire

Shell LiveWire provides information and advice for young entrepreneurs wanting to start their own business. Its annual awards are a showcase for young business talent, and are open to people aged between 16 and 30. An annual 'Young Entrepreneur of the Year' competition recognises the most successful and innovative. Awards totalling over £200,000, along with invaluable publicity, are available at local, regional and national heats. See http://www.shell-livewire.org/

Warning

What is not likely to be viewed as so appropriate by universities and employers alike is simply working for employment agencies on

> a self-employed basis, or simply 'minding' a business set up by other members of your friends, family, etc.

Operational positions

Sometimes students apply for jobs that are advertised as permanent positions but find that the firm will consider employing a student on a temporary contract. This is becoming more common, particularly with small and medium-sized enterprises (SMEs). Management may not have the resources to take on someone in a 'training' role; however, such positions can still offer valuable work experience although you might have to work a little harder in terms of creating your own agenda for development where this is possible.

It is difficult to say that such opportunities are in any way inferior to the traditional placement/training role. Often, 'real' jobs will provide very good experience of work and responsibility; perhaps the salary will be higher. To make things really work you need to explain clearly to the employer what experience you are looking for and discuss with them how this can best be achieved, whilst ensuring that the employer gets the required output from yourself.

As a minimum the employer needs to be aware from the outset that you will be supervised and that you will have an on-site visit from your placement tutor. Employers may also be required to fill in certain forms such as health and safety compliance and feedback reports on your progress. If this is made clear and put across positively at interview most employers will be happy to accommodate reasonable requests. The trick is to demonstrate that your development and appraisal are in the interests of both parties.

If it's any consolation, some jobs advertised as 'placement' positions can in reality be simply fill-in positions for vacancies for permanent staff and be extremely hard work. These need to be managed carefully.

Working for SMEs

Another trend in placements is the growing proportion of students working outside the traditional large companies, which tend to have well established and highly structured placement schemes. You need not be deterred from working for an SME on your placement year, especially if that's the best place to obtain the sort of technical, market sector or organisational experience that you want. However, there are several additional issues that you need to consider:

1 You may have to explain in your application and at interview what exactly a placement is all about and why it is of benefit for the company, to employ you in this manner. See application issues in Chapter 6 and the benefits of employing placement students in Appendix 3.
2 Health and safety procedures may not be so clear and formalised in very small companies and you should discuss this with your placement tutor and refer to the National Council for Work Experience (NCWE) Code of Good Practice at www.work-experience.org.
3 You may not be employed directly by the company: see below.

Working through employment agencies

Whilst you are very unlikely to be applying for placement jobs through employment agencies, when it comes to the contract of employment and getting paid you may end up not actually being employed directly by the company you are working for. This may seem somewhat strange but it is a consequence of the changing nature of employment practices that were mentioned in Chapter 1.

Many smaller companies which might be willing to employ young people on placement are concerned about administration and employment issues and employment agencies offer a form of protection from some (but not all) of those issues. Companies can sometimes have arbitrary restrictions on headcount from time to time (i.e., the number of people that individual departments are allowed to employ). As a result, companies both large and small are making increasing use of employment bureaus and temporary agencies to employ and pay staff. They then 'hire' staff from an agency for a weekly charge. To all intents and purposes, the employee works within the host company but is technically employed by a third party (the contract of employment is with the agency, not the company that you do work for).

The big disadvantage with such services is that you may not have the same employment rights as other people in the company that you are working for. Of course, this may not be too important since you will only be there for a relatively short time. The big advantage is that should your host company go into liquidation, and that can happen, you are more likely to get paid by a specialist employment agency than by an individual entrepreneur or small company. However, the opposite can also be true.

You may even be interviewed and selected by an independent company that recruits graduates and placement students on behalf of a client company, usually for the first stages of the selection process. This will make no difference to your eventual employment.

SUMMARY

We have looked at how the world of work is changing and opportunities to improve your competitive position by seeking a range of good quality work experience alongside your formal education. We have also looked at what constitutes good quality work experience and how, using an example of a part-time job, a lot of valuable evidence of skills and motivation can be demonstrated. Finally, we looked at some of the placement opportunities and formats that are available. In the next chapter we will look in detail at one of the emerging themes, *learning to learn*.

Reference

Handy, C.B. (1990) *The Age of Unreason*, Boston, MA: Harvard Business School Press.

3

Learning to learn and learning by doing

What I hear, I cannot remember
What I see, I do remember
What I do I understand

Chinese proverb

By the end of this chapter you will understand;

- the importance of a life-long approach to learning
- the process of learning and the importance of combining theory and practice
- what we mean by experiential learning and some of the key learning theories

INTRODUCTION: IT AIN'T WHAT YOU KNOW, IT'S THE WAY THAT YOU KNOW IT!

In Chapter 1 we have seen that to be an effective worker there is a wide range of skills to acquire. Many of those skills need to be gained through a combination of formal tuition (theory) and practical (work) experience. In terms of work experience you will largely have to take responsibility for your own learning. This chapter will look at the process of learning itself and the opportunities to learn through work and, indeed, continue learning throughout your life. The notion of life-long learning is a key theme of this book.

The process of learning can be complex and varied. We all learn in different ways, and in different ways at different times. This chapter will help you to identify what your preferred learning style is and to be aware of alternative styles. We will also consider how to explain your preferred learning style to a prospective employer and consider what learning opportunities might be available within a placement period.

In addition, we will look at some of the key theories on learning and then suggest how you might, first, gain suitable work experience and second, demonstrate a progressive attitude to a prospective employer in both reflecting on and learning from your experience. Obviously, it is difficult within a time-constrained interview for an employer to judge whether or not one candidate knows more than another. In any case, each employer's organisation is different. They will want you to learn their business and their approach, fast! At interview they will be more interested in the *how* rather than the *what* of learning.

THE NEED FOR A LIFE-LONG APPROACH TO LEARNING

The Dearing Report is presently the most significant and comprehensive single survey on the state and future of higher education in the UK. We have already referred to it in Chapter 1. This is what the report said about the skills that graduates would need in the future: 'Graduates, as a proportion of total employees, will continue to grow. They will need stronger inter-personal skills as well as intellectual rigour, and they will need to be life-long learners.'

What this means for all of us is listed below:

1   There will be more people of graduate level and ability competing for jobs.
2   Interpersonal skills, the ability to work with and influence other people, will be more important.
3   Also necessary will be the ability to analyse and evaluate new problems within a problem-solving framework using a broad base of established knowledge appropriate to the chosen field.
4   Skills and knowledge will rapidly become outdated and people must take responsibility for evaluating their own strengths and weaknesses and undertaking further learning as appropriate throughout their life.

There was a time when it was the employers' responsibility to identify development needs in their employees and then provide further training and learning. Progressive employers still do this of course, but nowadays in partnership with employees who wish to develop and improve them-selves. Many employers expect their employees to actually take the lead in identifying their own training needs and identifying appropriate opportunities. Note that funding for staff development is now often a resource that must be competed for.

The purpose in stating these things is that you will need to understand:

- what your learning needs might be
- how *you* learn best
- how to reflect on where you are now
- how to go about further learning

Surprisingly, whilst learning is something we've been doing since we were born, it doesn't always come naturally when the learning needs are complex, ill-defined and there are many different options for learning. It also is more difficult when the day-to-day pressures of study, work and life in general get in the way. Learning for life is a process that we need to learn how to do and employers will want you to show that you are indeed a self-motivated learner.

Figure 3.1 below shows the components of the learning process that we shall be coming in this chapter.

LEARNING AS A PROCESS: SOME DEFINITIONS

Herbert (1999) says: 'Knowledge is a noun, learning is a verb'. *Learning* is about doing (a process), and *knowledge* represents an accumulation of previous learning (facts, events and experiences).

Two definitions of learning are given below:

Get knowledge of, or skill in, by study, experience, or being taught. (*Oxford Dictionary*)

Any relatively permanent change in behaviour that can be attributed to experience. (Coon, 1995)

At school we mostly learn knowledge and techniques. Our knowledge is examined at the end of each course and then, with luck, we get a certificate saying that we have passed that subject. Each period of learning is well structured and organised by the tutor, with clear objectives and content that feed into the final test.

In real life there is often no such luxury, but that should not stop us learning. It often means that learning can be much more fun, although it can also be very frustrating and inefficient. In a moment we will look

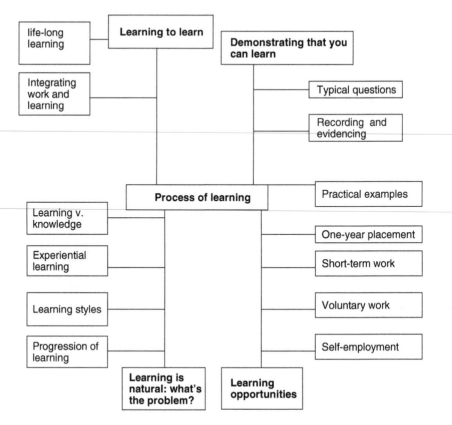

Figure 3.1 The process of learning

at some examples of your own learning but for now let's make sure that we understand the some of the terms in this area.

The difference between learning and knowledge may appear superficial: both are a part of education, so use that term to be on the safe side. However, many job applicants make the mistake of simply detailing lots of things they know rather than putting these into a wider context of learning and development. Let's have a look at what knowledge is all about.

THE BUILD-UP OF KNOWLEDGE

Figure 3.2 provides an illustration of this:

1 The term '*data*' relates to facts, events, transactions, etc. For example, a sales invoice contains a number of data fields such as the customer's

name and account number; the goods value; the delivery date; and so on.

2   *Information* is data that has been processed in such a way that it has meaning and relevance to the person who receives it. For example, an analysis of sales in a certain region provides information to the sales manager for the purpose of monitoring the performance of the sales team. However, the distinction between data and information can sometimes become blurred, dependent on the perspective of the user.

Information can have significant monetary value. Credit referencing agencies such as Dunn & Bradstreet, or the British company, Experian, are good examples of companies which earn money through the collection and management of vast quantities of data about people's financial profiles. These data are then processed, interpreted and sold as information in the form of credit ratings.

3   *Knowledge* is slightly more difficult to define, but is generally taken to represent the collection of events, experiences and feelings. Knowledge is comprised of two elements:

(a)   *explicit* knowledge, such as facts, transactions and events; that is, things that can be precisely and clearly expressed (in terms of management information systems, such knowledge can be codified, categorised and stored);

(b)   *tacit* knowledge, which is implied or inferred. It concerns the experiences and feelings that exist in people's minds.

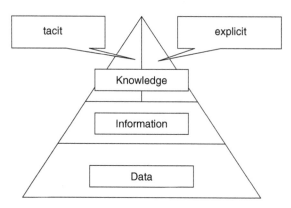

Figure 3.2   The pyramid of knowledge 1

The significance of these terms will become clearer a bit further on when we look at Bloom's taxonomy of learning and how to document your experiences. Let's now look at some examples of how we learn.

SO HOW DO I LEARN?

You may be asking yourself many questions at this stage. If learning is so important then how should I do it? I've been learning things all my life; learning is natural so why should I need to study it? Employers can soon figure out what I've learnt if they want!

Well, maybe it's not quite that straightforward. Let's have a closer look at how we learn and let's do that by doing!

Activity

Think of TWO things that you have previously learnt to do, such as: riding a bike; playing a musical instrument; mastering a new computer game; learning a new topic at school, etc.

Describe how you went about the task and why you ultimately succeeded or failed. (Don't worry if your examples didn't work out as planned; we often learn more from our mistakes than from the things that work out right.) You might find the following prompts helpful.

Prompts for activity

		Challenge 1		Challenge 2
I wanted to do it because . . .				
My first step was . . .				
How did I do?				
What I did next				
How did I get better?				
How did I know I'd got better?				
How did I master it?				
What kept me going?				
For examples see the end of this chapter, but first try to have a go yourself.				

Activity

Now suggest how your learning process might have been better.

Activity

Now describe how you would suggest someone else might tackle this challenge. Think here about whether your advice might be different for different members of your family or friends.

Activity

Now think about how you learn new things (knowledge and techniques) at university. Is this different, and if so why is that the case?

Reflection

Let's now examine what you have just done.

You have probably chosen challenges that involved trying things out before relating experience to theory, rather than first studying the theory and then doing the task. Most of our formal learning, at school and university, tends to start with theory and then moves on to practice. But at which point do you prefer to start? If you've ever watched someone tackling the construction of flat-pack furniture you'll have noticed that some people first read all the instructions thoroughly, whilst others might start by picking up the pieces and trying to see what fits where, referring to the instructions when they get stuck.

The process of learning is made up of different phases and we can choose to start at different points. A new cycle of learning often starts through doing or experiencing something. This is called *experiential* learning.

EXPERIENTIAL LEARNING: THE KOLB LEARNING CYCLE

Much of the writings in this area are based on the work of David A. Kolb (1984), who created a model based on four discrete stages: concrete experience, observation and reflection, the formation of abstract concepts, and testing in new situations. This is represented as a circle of learning as shown in Figure 3.3:

1 *Experiencing,* or *the 'doing'* of a task, is the first stage in which the individual, team or organization simply carries out the task assigned. The doing person is usually not reflecting on the task at this time, but carrying it out with intention.

2 *Reflection* involves stepping back from task involvement and *reviewing what has been done* and experienced. Skills of analysis and recording are key. It is important not to bias the observation with your existing views.

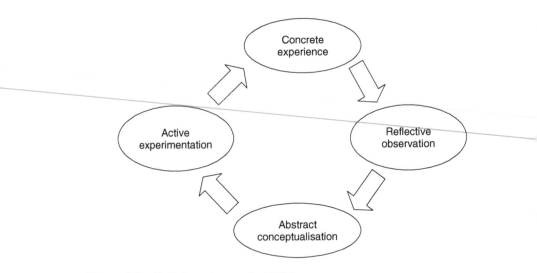

Figure 3.3 Kolb learning cycle (1984)

3   *Conceptualisation* involves *interpreting the events* that have been observed and *understanding the relationships* among them. It is at this stage that external theories may be particularly helpful for framing and explaining events. This enables a new understanding of the situation and translates it into *predictions* about what is likely to happen next or *what actions should be taken* to refine the way the task is handled.

4   *Experimentation* tests the assumptions and starts the cycle again.

Kolb suggests that the learning cycle can begin at any one of the four points, and that it should really be viewed as a continuous circle. However, in practice the learning process often begins with a person carrying out a particular action and then observing and reflecting on the effect of the action. Sometimes this is not practical or advisable, (say, in the planning of a new traffic system or a new medical procedure).

The next step is to understand the effect(s) so that if the same action were taken in the same circumstances it would be possible to anticipate what would follow from the action (cause and effect). The third step tries to understand the general principle involved. Finally, this theory would be tested through further experimentation.

Often the eventual failure of the challenge results from making repeated mistakes or an inability to learn from experience. The cycle is based on the idea that the more often we reflect on a task, the more often we have the opportunity to modify and refine our efforts.

Each of these learning activities can be divided into opposites. For example some people best perceive information using concrete experiences (such as feeling, touching, seeing and hearing) while others best perceive information abstractly (using mental or visual conceptualisation).

Whilst we often start by simply doing or experiencing something, the examples of your own learning challenges included two other dimensions: motivation and planning (see Figure 3.4 overleaf). Let's incorporate these into an expanded and somewhat simplified learning cycle. We'll then try a couple of further challenges which you might use at interview if asked to explain how you might approach something new.

EXAMPLE OF THE LEARNING PROCESS

Let's consider a very simple example to demonstrate this process using some of the terms above:

Motivation: feeling hungry, need something to eat
Plan: to get into the snack bar
Action: try to push open the snack bar door
Feedback: door doesn't move

Reflection: Hey, what's happening here?
            Questions   Is snack bar open?
                                  Does door open another way?
                                  Has my watch stopped?
            Information search Are the lights on? Are people inside?
                                  Have opening hours changed (see side of door)?
                                  Does door handle say pull?
Thinking/   Try pulling the door. If that doesn't work, come back later.
Experimentation

Whatever the result, I will have learnt to apply an alternative *technique* (pulling the door), or else I will have learnt a new *fact* that will stop me wasting time in the future (the snack bar opens later/staff are all off sick). Or perhaps I will develop an alternative plan, and go to the nearest shop or vending machine.

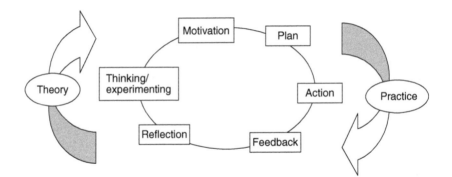

Figure 3.4 Expanded learning cycle

Source: Adapted from Kolb (1984).

Activity

Pick TWO further examples of learning challenges, preferably things you might have encountered in previous work experience or in education. Use the headings below to help you analyse your learning experiences. See example at end of chapter.

Prompts for activity

Wanting

What was your motivation: why did you want to do it?
What was your objective: what did you want to achieve?

Planning

What was your target timescale: how long did you expect to take?
What research did you do: how did you find out how to do it?
What tuition support was required: who did you ask?
What other support was available: did your friends help you?

Action

What learning activities did you do?
How did you actually learn?

Feedback

How did you assess your progress: how did you know how you were doing?
What benchmarks did you use: how were you doing compared to your friends?
What feedback did you seek: did you ask anyone else how you were doing?

Reflection

Was your learning a success?
Could you still be better at your task: what aspects could you improve?
Could you have learnt quicker or better if you had done things differently?

Thinking

How can you improve?
How could you be the best in the world at whatever it is?

LEARNING STYLES

When you have to learn something new you probably approach the task in a similar fashion each time. That is, over time you have developed a pattern of behaviour that you use for new learning. This pattern is called a *learning style*, which describes the attitudes and behaviours that determine our preferred way of learning.

While we don't approach every new learning task in exactly the same way each of us tends to develop a set of behaviours that we are most comfortable with. If we get to know those behaviour patterns we can see when they are helpful and when they are not.

From the last activity you might have already identified a preference in terms of how you learn. Other people might have different styles and you will need to be aware of this when working in teams. The next sections will consider:

- what your preferred style is
- when it might be appropriate to change your style
- how to explain your style to employers and ensure that your stated style does not unduly contradict the results of any assessment tests they might ask you to do

The four learning preferences of Honey and Mumford (1986) based upon the Kolb learning cycle are as follows:

Activist	Prefers doing and experimenting.
	Likes to have a go to see what happens.
Reflector	Observes and then reflects.
	Likes to gather information and mull things over.
Theorist	Wants to understand underlying reasons, concepts and relationships.
	Likes to tidy up and reach some conclusions.
Pragmatist	Likes to 'have a go' to try to work things out first to see if/how they work.
	Likes tried and tested techniques that are relevant to own problems.

You may already have seen a tendency towards one or more of these styles from the analysis of your previous learning challenges. A person playing the piano or mastering the computer game would be strong in the activist and pragmatist categories.

Activity

Look at your own learning examples and try to categorise your own learning style. Which of the four styles best describes your approach?

Note that you may well use a different approach for different types of activity.

Example of learning approach

Let's assume that a another person John also learnt to play the piano. John approached the challenge in his own way; this is what he said.

I looked at all the keys on the piano and thought that there must be some structure to them. Why are some white and others are black? What makes the noise and is it like a guitar which seems easier to understand? How is sheet music organised? It again seems totally incomprehensible but surely must have some structure.

My approach was to look inside the piano and watch what happened when I hit some of the keys. I then got a book on music and read that. This helped me to understand the structure of the music and how things like timing and pitch are organised. About two weeks later I finally had a go at playing some simple scales and then tunes on the piano. I had to know how it all worked before I felt comfortable doing it.

John's preferred style would seem closest to the reflector and theorist styles. Note that we don't go so far as to say John's style is definitively only one style out of the four. He has elements of all four styles. He hit the keys to see what happened, for example, but essentially his major leanings are towards a combination of two styles, reflector and theorist.

Case study

This example might sound a bit extreme but it nicely illustrates the point that learning experiences can be approached very differently.

In the late 1990s, one large electricity company decided to launch a scheme to get its employees more familiar with personal computers and encourage the use of e-mail. Amongst a number of learning initiatives it made available a home personal computer with Internet subscription at a nominal charge to a large number of key employees. The scheme was first trialled with office-based staff with great success and then 'rolled out' to the engineers. Whilst the second phase had some success it also met a few problems. At first there were a number of inexplicable hardware failures which (it turned out) were caused by these technical staff opening up the computers and fiddling about with them! Then in the longer term it appeared that some engineers were not using the computers because they just didn't see the benefit of e-mail: they had paper systems and the telephone which had worked well for years.

The organisers of the scheme realised that whereas the problem with office staff was fear of the technology (they could easily appreciate the benefits), the engineers were intrigued by the technology but couldn't see the use for it. They had no motivation and a different way of approaching learning (theorist rather than pragmatist). The learning cycle and an appreciation of learning styles would have helped greatly in designing the scheme.

Honey and Mumford learning styles analysis

As can be seen in the case study, it can be of great benefit for organisations to understand how people learn when developing their staff. It can also help them to ensure that they recruit namely people of a certain type, workers who will fit in with the rest of the workforce or who can adapt their learning styles to suit different situations. The main contribution to analysis of learning styles is by Honey and Mumford (1986), and you may well come across tests at interviews that have been based upon their ideas, and we advise you to consult this work.

Activity

To analyse your own learning style see the *Manual of Learning Styles* (Honey and Mumford). Your placement office, careers service or learning support unit is likely to be able to provide you with a copy. Alternatively, go to the following web site and take the on-line test, although there is now a £10 charge for doing this!

www.peterhoney.com

Does your result correspond with your own thoughts?

Types of learner

Based on the categories of the cycle we can identify four basic learning approaches:

Type I learner: You are primarily a 'hands-on' learner. You tend to rely on intuition rather than logic. You like to rely on other people's analysis rather than your own. You enjoy applying your learning in real life situations.

Type II learner: You like to look at things from many points of view. You would rather watch rather than take action. You like to gather information and create many categories for things. You like using your imagination in problem-solving. You are very sensitive to feelings when learning.

Type III learner: You like solving problems and finding practical solutions and uses for your learning. You shy away from social and interpersonal issues and prefer technical tasks.

Type IV learner: You are concise and logical. Abstract ideas and concepts are more important to you than people issues. Practicality is less important to you than a good logical explanation.

OTHER VIEWS OF LEARNING: TOP-DOWN OR BOTTOM-UP

Some people are *top-down* learners and look at the whole task (random), while *bottom-up* learners proceed one step at a time (sequentially). Which approach best describes your own?

How did you start reading this book? From the beginning, starting with the preface, or did you dive into the bit about CV writing and move on to this bit as you needed to understand more?

A STAIRWAY OF LEARNING: BLOOM'S TAXONOMY

Another influential theory in the area of learning and critical thinking models is *Bloom's taxonomy of higher thinking*. Bloom (1956) categorised thinking into the six stages shown in Figure 3.5. We have depicted the taxonomy as a pyramid whereby the building blocks of knowledge are made sense of allowing judgements to be made. Note how this builds upon figure 3.2 shown earlier. You may not be aware of it but Bloom's model is central to the design of curricula, teaching and assessment methods in many schools, colleges and universities. You will see links with the structure of knowledge earlier in the chapter.

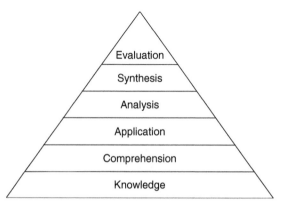

Figure 3.5   The pyramid of knowledge 2

Let us have a closer look at these terms starting with the 'building blocks' of knowledge:

Knowledge	To know something means to have a fact or bit of information at your disposal. One can 'know' something without understanding it or being able to put it into a higher context. For example, we might know that there is a topic of regression analysis in statistics without knowing what it means.
Comprehension	To comprehend a fact or piece of information is to understand what it means. For example, we might understand that regression analysis enables us to see correlations between sets of data.
Application	To apply information means to find some practical use for it. Using regression analysis we might determine how the costs of the factory go up or down as the level of production fluctuates.
Analysis	To analyse means to break information down into the sum of its parts and to see how those parts work together. We might use regression analysis in deciding how much our products actually cost to make.
Synthesis	To synthesise means to take the knowledge you have and connect it with other knowledge. For example, how do product costings relate to the present sales prices we could charge? What price might we be able to charge in future?
Evaluation	To evaluate means to be able to judge. Should we quote the customer that price? Was regression analysis the right technique to apply? Are there alternatives? Have we the knowledge or the time to re-evaluate the problem?

Note the similarity of this progression with the hierarchy of knowledge described earlier. The acquisition of knowledge is the starting point for learning.

Activity

Write down an example of your own learning in each stage in the taxonomy of learning. Do this first for school or university activities and then for your past work experience.

See the end of this chapter for an example.

Knowledge	
Comprehension	
Application	
Analysis	
Synthesis	

Evaluation

PUTTING THE THEORY INTO PRACTICE: EXAMPLES

So, if you now appreciate that we can learn things in different ways and that even the act of thinking about something has different stages, how do you put that into practice to help your placement planning?

1　By thinking about your past work experience and learning style.
2　Preparing to record this in your CV.

Activity

1　If you haven't already done so, make a record of what skills, knowledge and experience you have gained in your previous work experience.
2　What specifically did you have to learn how to do?
3　How did you learn this?
4　Did you have control over how you learnt or were you trained/ instructed in a certain manner?
5　What learning skills do you think a future employer will expect you to have?
6　How do you think you can acquire/evidence those skills?
7　Do you they fit with your natural learning style?

Note: for items 2–4 you may choose to select just 3–4 examples.

Examples of learning activity

Think of something you have learnt to do, such as playing a musical instrument; riding a bike; conquering a difficult computer game; etc.

	Playing the piano	*Computer game*
I wanted to do it because …	I'd always wanted to.	I'd done the first version.
	I'd heard other people play.	My mates had all got it.
	I might become rich and famous.	It was just me against the machine!
My first step was …	To have a go – just messing about.	Bought the game, loaded it up then tried to figure it out.
	Someone showed me how to play 'Chopsticks'.	
How did I do?	Awful – it's impossible.	Couldn't get past level 1. Couldn't understand the rules/options.
What I did next	Joined music lessons at school.	Read the instructions.
		Watched my mates. Bought a magazine that gave tips.
How did I get better?	Practice.	Practice.
	Learnt to read music.	Found the 'cheats' on the Internet.
How did I know I'd got better?	It sounded better.	Got through more levels.
	Eventually, I could do two different things with my hands at the same time (or in different times!). People said I'd got better.	Achieved higher scores.
How did I master it?	Practice, practice, practice!	Practice, practice, practice!

	Had professional lessons. Joined a band. Listened carefully to other people/went to concerts.	
What kept me going?	Determination not to be beaten.	Determination not to be beaten.
	Encouragement from family and friends. Entered for music exams.	Needed to beat my mates.

Now suggest how your learning process might have been better.

Perhaps if I'd learnt at the same time as with a friend or gone to lessons sooner I might have made faster progress and not picked up some bad habits that I'm now struggling to forget! I'd make a plan so that I could keep a check on my progress and not be tempted to do too much too fast and get disheartened.

Now describe how you would suggest someone else might tackle this challenge. Think here about whether your advice might be different for different members of your family or friends.

I'd advise them to set a target within a timescale that is achievable but will nevertheless push them a bit, (e.g., play a certain piece of music). My dad would want to start with how the piano worked and how it made the different sounds – he'd probably take it to bits before he started playing it then read everything about learning to play the piano that he could find. My sister would probably want to start with another instrument like a recorder first and be competent at reading music before she started to play.

Example of work experience

Entered a competition with a school friend to do a business plan.

Wanting   **What was your motivation: why did you want to do it?**
£50 worth of book tokens was one good reason but in any case I've always been interested in business and I might want to start my own architects' practice one day.

What was your objective: what did you want to achieve?

Win the prize and learn about things such as preparing a marketing plan and dealing with a bank (a bank was sponsoring the competition and would give advice to the shortlisted entries).

Planning **What was your target timescale: how long did you expect to take?**

Had to be done by 30 November so we started in early September.

We made a list of all the component parts we had to produce, the research necessary and then we worked backwards from the end to do one task per week.

What research did you do: how did you find out how to do it?

Searched the world wide web. Found a good explanations and example businesses on the Royal Bank of Scotland site (www.rbs.com). Found book by Richard Stutely in the library – very helpful.

What tuition support was required: who did you ask?

The local bank manager came to school to give us some advice and we also asked the accounting teacher to look at our financial projections.

What other support was available: did your friends help you?

Other friends were also doing the competition but we agreed that we would pool our basic research if not our actual ideas. At the end we also read through each other's plans and made suggestions as everyone was finding it quite difficult.

Doing **What learning activities did you do?**

We read a lot of the information we had found on the web and in books but we started to get confused because everything was a lot more detailed than we really needed and we couldn't agree where to start and what was most important.

How did you actually learn?

It was hard to get going as it was a big task.

In the end we just started trying to writing the marketing plan which made us focus on understanding what was involved in marketing and realise all the things that we didn't yet know. We made a huge list of all the specific things we had to do and divided the tasks up between us. We also discovered that we needed to know more about writing spreadsheets and so we had to improve our IT skills by referring to a manual.

Feedback **How did you assess your progress: how did you know how you were doing?**
We had to revise the plan a few times but we ticked off each job as we did them and this involved reading each other's work before we were satisfied with it.
What benchmarks did you use: how were you doing compared to your friends?
It was difficult to know how we were really doing as everyone was being very cagey about exactly what they were doing.
What feedback did you seek: did you ask anyone else how you were doing?
I asked my mum to read through. She didn't understand a lot of it which was good in that she asked a lot of questions and so we took out or explained a lot of the jargon that we'd used.

Reflection **Was your learning a success?**
We didn't win the prize. Apparently, we were third out of 30 entries so top 10%. We did learn a lot and one day I might just do it!
Could you still be better at your task: what aspects could you improve?
One thing that became apparent was that between us we both had very different approaches to word-processing. Different ways of doing the headings and page set up, etc. When we put our two parts together we got into a bit of a mess and so I'm going to use a more structured approach in future.
Could you have learnt quicker or better if you had done things differently?
Again to do with structure. Once the whole plan got bigger than about 15 pages we started to get very muddled as to what we had covered and where, and what we had to do. We ended doing some jobs twice, which was inefficient. We needed to plan things better from the outset.

Thinking **How can you improve?**
Write down the lessons from this job before I forget.
Practice doing large tasks like this.
How could you be the best in the world at whatever it is?
More practice. Do a module in business studies next semester.

Example: taxonomy of learning

First example based on an academic scenario, assessing own work experience

Knowledge First I learnt about the major theories of learning (e.g., Kolb's learning cycle and Honey and Mumford's learning styles).

Comprehension Next I saw how these could be applied in a hypothetical example of work experience.

Application Then I applied the learning theories to a couple of examples of my own learning challenges.

Analysis Perhaps the next thing I need to do is to look at my whole work and education to date and break it down into each aspect of the theories to see if my experience of learning is sufficiently comprehensive.
Task: to go through each theory and identify an example from my own experience.

Synthesis Prepare a table of my experience of learning and compare this to my friends' experience and the expectations of employers.

Evaluation Ask myself what gaps exist in my knowledge and how significant these are in terms of the whole picture. Decide whether further action is necessary.

Second example based on work experience in the department store

Knowledge	Learnt many of the product line codes.
Comprehension	Understood how the coding structure was related to departments or types of goods.
Application	Used my knowledge of the codes to correct or query requests from departments that didn't seem correct.
Analysis	Had to understand the exact situation by careful analysis of all the relevant information when shop floor managers complained about stock shortages or wrong goods being delivered.
Synthesis	Had to assimilate a number of different viewpoints and versions of events.
Evaluation	Had to make a decision as to whether to put through the request as an emergency order or refer to the stores supervisor.

Note: we are probably stretching this one a little bit for a 6 week job but, hopefully, you can appreciate how a structured approach to learning can be shown in what at first sight might seem to be an extremely mundane job!

References

Bloom, B.S. (1956) *Taxonomy of educational objectives. Handbook 1: cognitive domain*, Harlow: Longman.

Brookfield, S.D. (1983) *Adult Learning, Adult Education and the Community*, Milton Keynes: Open University Press.

Coon, D. (1995) *Introduction to Psychology: Exploration and Application*, 7th edn, West.

Dearing, R., (1997) *National Committee of Enquiry into HE*, London: HMSO.

Herbert, I. (1999) 'Knowledge is a noun, leaning is a verb', *Management Accounting*, 78 (2), Chartered Institute of Management Accountants.

Honey, P. and Mumford, A. (1986) *The Manual of Learning Styles*, Maidenhead: Peter Honey, www.peterhoney.com.

Kolb, D.A. (1984) *Experiential Learning: Experience as the Source of Learning and Development*, Englewood Cliffs, NJ: Prentice Hall.

Stutely, R. (2002) *The Definitive Business Plan: The Fast-track to Intelligent Business Planning for Executives and Entrepreneurs*, 2nd edn, London: Prentice Hall.

4

A framework for skills development

By the end of this chapter you should be able to:

- understand what we mean by transferable skills
- plan your development using the PINT framework of skills (see below for an explanation)
- analyse and develop a range of personal and interpersonal skills
- record your skills with evidence, both prior to placement, and in the work place.

INTRODUCTION: AFTER THE 3 RS IT'S SKILL, SKILLS, SKILLS

Before we move into the process of job hunting in Chapters 5 and 6, let us reconsider what employers are looking for in addition to the subject-specific, technical competences of your individual degree programme. Generally, these are as follows:

1 Qualities of character (maturity, honesty, etc.).
2 Aptitudes that will enable you to learn to do the job quickly and do it competently (intelligence, reasoning ability, etc.).
3 A range of what are called transferable skills that can be learnt through study and experience and which are necessary to a greater or lesser

extent in most work situations (communication, team working, ICT, number, etc.).

A major challenge for students (and, indeed, for tutors and employers) can be defining what we mean by these general skills and what to call them. There is no easy answer. This chapter introduces a range of core ideas in this area and it is anticipated that you will read more on this important subject for yourself. There are a number of very useful references in the final chapter.

Many universities provide help with study skills and there is inevitably some overlap with some of the transferable skills that we shall be covering in this text. Our approach is to look at the skills that you will need in the work place so that you can prepare your job applications with these in mind. You should also find this chapter useful when actually at work to apply and record skills.

Note

You need to be aware that many texts approach this matter from a single preferred position. We shall make no prescriptions in this book. We will, for the sake of simplicity, briefly discuss some of the main approaches and then suggest a set of terms within a framework that will then be used throughout this book. You should appreciate that in further reading different terms and interpretations should be seen as enrichment of your understanding rather than as a source of unnecessary confusion.

The confusion over terms, definitions and content is best illustrated through an extract from A. Woollard, a former Head of the UK Government's Higher Education Quality Division:

All the words used in core-skills-talk do raise potential problems if one attempts to define them too closely. What do we really mean by 'core' – core of what? Is 'transferability' a rigorously valid concept? And how can we talk legitimately about 'skills' once we get beyond the purely routine? However, since I am by origin a theologian, I do not personally have much of a problem with discourse, which begs questions if taken literally but which still may point to something important.

To structure your preparation for placement and your learning whilst at work this chapter will present a framework of skills for placement which we've called 'PINT'. We will explain below how to develop some of the key personal and interpersonal skills (see Figure 4.1).

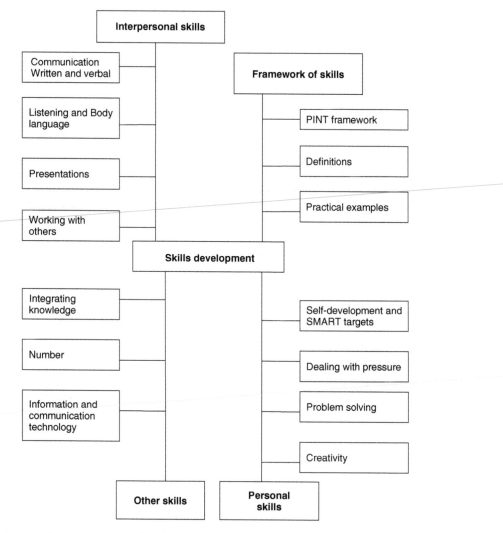

Figure 4.1 Framework for skills development

PINT = Personal, Interpersonal, Number & Technical skills framework.
SMART = Specific, Measurable, Achievable, Realistic, Time-bound.

DISCUSSION OF TERMS

There are numerous terms in current usage to describe those skills beyond the capability solely to apply the technical aspects of a discipline.

In describing the notion of an employable person the term 'graduateness' is often used but seldom defined.

The following section discusses some of these terms since you may come across them in further reading and in your job hunting.

In Chapter 1 we cited the Dearing Report as evidence that employers seek a wide range of skills. The report grouped these skills into three categories: (traditional) 'academic skills'; 'personal development skills'; and 'enterprise skills'. Inevitably, there is some overlap between these three categories.

Table 1.1 showed the skills that employers say they need from higher education over the next 10–20 years. Some of the skills, such as 'flexibility', are difficult to define but that doesn't mean that they are any less important. Employers find it difficult to express exactly what they are looking for; it often reflects the present context of the organisation and personal view of the individual recruiter. Sometimes it is simply a reaction to the last person employed who wasn't a success. Below are interview extracts from a couple of managers looking to recruit graduates into accounting posts.

Case study 1

A lot of the people who we've got have come through the graduate scheme do accounting degrees. It gives a quick start into a career and they are able to use skills at an early stage. I think what I notice is that the people who are particularly strong and make a big contribution as a graduate are those who have done some form of placement year so they have got the combination of practical experience and the theory.

The degree is a good starting point but we test people more in the Assessment Centre, on their personality, on things like communication skills and showing that they can develop arguments and think logically. We need to be satisfied that they have got the capability to produce business reports, and we do test their numerical reasoning and verbal skills. So the accounting degree is useful, it does give a good background, but it's not a prerequisite.

The way we work it is that we have a 1 1/2 day Assessment Centre. This consists of an afternoon of group exercises, then an evening session of the Company giving presentations to them and then, the following day, there would be an applicant presentation, interview and then verbal and numerical reasoning tests.

Case study 2

And interpersonal skills, what are you looking for there?

I think there it's very much people that show ability for thought and commitment. People who can go out and actually know what they want to do and go out and achieve as well. So people that have taken gap years and done something constructive with it would obviously attract us to them rather than somebody who has done nothing.
And those qualities and traits would be identified in the interviewing behaviour?

Absolutely. Some of the skills we are looking for there are coping with ambiguity; teamwork; self-motivation and achievement.

Notice the different perspectives but also the similarities. The relevance of the degree subject seems less important than the skills. The second manager is much keener on prior achievement and specifically cites a gap year as a way of evidencing this. Many recruiters will say that skills are difficult to define but will also say that it's pretty clear when you have someone in front of you that has the right skills. No doubt there is some truth in this, although on the other hand it's not much use to job hunters like yourself.

Core skills

Perhaps the pre-eminent demonstration in the area of so-called transferable core skills is the National Council for Vocational Qualifications (NCVQ), where the following groups of skills are identified: communication, application of number, IT, problem-solving, working with others, and improving one's own learning and performance.

Another term in popular usage is 'soft' skills.

A FRAMEWORK OF SKILLS FOR PLACEMENT

Transferable skills is the preferred term for use in this book. We simply mean *any skill that is not discipline-specific and can be learnt in one situation and applied in another.* For example, using a surveyor's theodolite is useful in surveying tasks but of no use in, say, making textiles, whereas the ability to communicate effectively between people is likely to be useful in both situations. It is a key issue for employers and you should make every effort to develop your skills and take every opportunity to convince a future employer that you are competent in as many aspects as possible. The following quotation is again taken from the Dearing Report; it is a statement given by an employer to the inquiry which is typical of many others: *'The[re are] falling standards of numeracy, grammar and interpersonal awareness [in applicants] as identified through our graduate programme selection process.'*

There are many reference sources available to help you and a selection of these are given at the end of the chapter. In this book we shall use the acronym PINT as a framework of skills to allow you to identify those areas for development and monitor your progress before during and after placement.

Personal Skills	Self-development and learning
Interpersonal skills	Communication + working with and relating to others
Knowledge and number	Integration of academic knowledge with practice.
Technology	Mainly the appreciation and application of ICT

To complete the analogy of your personal pint pot, filling up with skills, we shall imagine the head of the pint bursting with the bubbles of your character and personality – your own *va va voom*! See Figure 4.2.

This framework should not be seen as an exhaustive checklist for job-hunting preparation, or even as the measure of the perfect placement. It should be viewed primarily as a structure for students in preparing CVs

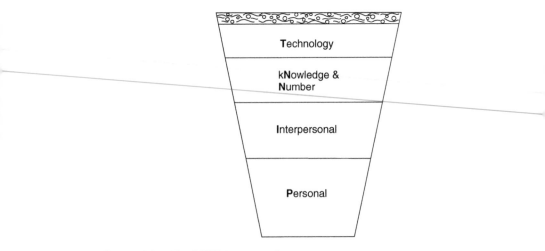

Figure 4.2   The PINT framework

and application forms, either before or after placement, and for their employers in planning the direction and progress of the placement. This chapter will cover personal skills, interpersonal skills, knowledge and number, and technology. Two important aspects of interpersonal skills, assertiveness and negotiation, are covered in Chapter 8, as these skills can often difficult to relate to whilst actually in education but will more than likely be needed in the work place.

The table framework in the tinted panel will help you to audit (take stock of) your present situation and record your progress before placement. A version with an example of placement experience appears in Chapter 8 and copies for you to print and complete for yourself are on the web site.

	Examples of Experience/Accomplishment
Personal Skills	
Self-management	
• Setting personal objectives	
• Creating a work programme	
• Time management	
• Working to deadlines	
• Coping with stress	
Self-Development	
• Creativity	
• Problem solving	
• Ability to reflect on and learn from experience	
• Critical assessment of progress towards objectives	
Interpersonal Skills	
Communication	
• Writing reports	
memos (internal)	
letters (external)	
note taking	

• Verbal speaking	
listening (comprehension)	
feedback	
• Body language	
• Presentations structure and use of visual aids	
audience contact	
handling questions	
Working with and relating to others	
• Negotiation	
• Personal assertiveness	
• Dealing with customers/clients	
• Handling queries	
• Working as part of a team	
• Task management	
KNowledge and Number	
Integration of subject knowledge from studies	
Exposure to other disciplines/areas of business	
Use of numerical data	
Technology – Information and Communication	
• Word-processing	
• Spreadsheets	
• Presentation package	
• Databases	
• E-mail systems	
• E-commerce/The Internet	
• Specific applications such as scientific packages, business systems, etc.	

PERSONAL SKILLS

Now, to get your pint pot filling up with skills, let's begin with personal skills.

Employers will want to see evidence that you are capable of managing yourself as well as other people but, perhaps more importantly, whilst advice will abound, you have to take responsibility for managing your own career and that process starts with preparation for placement. Most people will change jobs a number of times during their working lives and few will escape redundancy during that time. You may have a period of time in self-employment.

Charles Handy, the eminent writer on organisations and personnel management, talks about the portfolio worker as a new breed of individual who will manage his own career and build up a portfolio of skills and knowledge that he will 'sell' to a number of employers throughout his career. Even in Japan, the idea of life-time employment with a single company is being challenged by corporations who must adjust to more flexible patterns of operation. In the next section we will look at some aspects of self-management.

Self-management

Setting personal objectives	What do you want to achieve? This may go well beyond the immediate objectives and perhaps be on a 5 or even 10 year timescale (see more in Chapter 5; see also SMART targets below).
Creating a work programme	Can you plan your work activities over a number of weeks or months? If your employer is new to the idea of placements then you may need to suggest your own programme once you have settled in. See SMART targets below.
Time management	This is a whole subject in itself; despite the popular perception it is not simply about being able to shave on the way to work and buying ready-peeled vegetables or speed reading techniques.

Whilst saving seconds from all aspects of your daily routines can be important, time management also encompasses a more fundamental and holistic approach |

	to setting priorities and balancing your life between work, play and people. For more information see the final chapter.
Working to deadlines	Obviously, you will say 'Yes, of course I can', but you need to acknowledge the difficulties sometimes and be prepared to provide examples of your success.
Coping with stress	An increasing factor in modern life, and not just at work. Again there is much advice on this and some useful references are given in Chapter 10.

Setting SMART targets

Soon it will be time to start planning for your placement or to acquire further part-time work experience before you start applying for placement jobs. Depending on where you are in the placement process there will be a number of things that you need to be planning for and there are some further suggestions in Chapter 5. To finish off this chapter on learning and development we suggest that your planning should be based around SMART targets. These are:

Specific	Do your targets say exactly what it is you need to do?
Measurable	Can you show proof that you have achieved your targets?
Achievable	Are your targets easy enough to achieve in the time you have been given?
Realistic	Are your targets things that you can really do something about?
Time-bound	Have you decided dates for achieving your targets?

Note

You may come across slight variations to these. One version substitutes 'Manageable' and 'Assessable', but the overall effect is the same.

Self-development

The modern world moves increasingly fast. To succeed in the long term you will need to continually update your knowledge, your skills and your plans. That means developing a capacity for life-long learning. Again, it's about accepting change and making plans to update yourself to cope with those changes. Below are a few headings that might be useful in terms of thinking about self-improvement. They are not end products in themselves but skills that you can apply to new situations and challenges.

Creativity	To what extent can you think in original ways? Can you generate ideas and new opportunities?
Problem solving	Can you use a problem-solving framework to analyse problems and generate solutions? See below.
Ability to reflect on and learn from experience	Do you learn from experience? Do you continually analyse what you are doing and try to make things better? Are you a life-long learner? (The detail of this was covered in Chapter 3.)
Critical assessment of progress towards objectives	Do you regularly assess your own progress and set new targets? What action do you take to remedy your weaknesses?

Problem-solving and decision-making

Problem-solving is the whole process of identifying a problem (the symptoms and its causes), then gathering and analysing data before proposing solutions and choosing between the alternatives. A decision can be defined as a judgement, conclusion or resolution reached or given. Put more simply, it is the act of making up one's mind. Note that the term 'decision-making' is often used to infer the whole process of analysing problems, proposing alternative solutions and then choosing between alternatives, but it is really a sub-section of problem-solving.

A problem-solving framework

Identify the problem	What is exactly the problem to be solved? Why should it be solved?
Gather information	What factors does the problem involve? What has caused the problem?
Brainstorm possible solutions	Generate ideas for possible solutions.
Identify the criteria to judge the alternatives	What standards and criteria should the solution meet?
Evaluate the best alternative	Consider each choice in terms of its consequences and payback.
Make your decision	Which is best?

Implement the decision   Use a plan of action with clear steps.
Evaluate the outcome of your   What lessons can be learnt? Is there still
decision and actions   a problem? If so, return to step 1 and
                                       repeat the process.

INTERPERSONAL SKILLS

Communication

The ability to communicate clearly and concisely to other human beings
is the key skill set in any vocation. However, some aspects may not been
covered during the formal education and it is difficult to simulate real
business scenarios. Good communication at work involves being able to
relate to people from different backgrounds and age groups from your
own. Don't worry unduly, though: people at work will be tolerant whilst
you learn these things, so long as you appear willing to listen and to
learn.

In our experience it is communication skills that are most often cited
by employers as problematic with student employees. In this section we
will look at the process of communication and explain some of its forms.

The communication process

Effective communication only exists when a message is received, understood, accepted and correctly acted upon. The process is about transferring
knowledge, changing opinions and issuing instructions.

The communication process can be seen in Figure 4.3.

A message must be clear, unambiguous and understandable to the
receiver. It is important to understand the position and background of

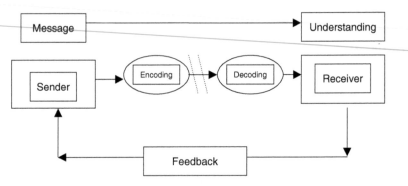

Figure 4.3   Model of communication
Source: Adapted from Shannon and Weaver (1949).

the person(s) receiving the message. It is essential to direct the message to the right person(s) in a form that allows them to access it *physically*.

It must also be *psychologically* acceptable. Cultural background plays an important part in communications, and what is acceptable in one culture may be taboo or even illegal in another.

Feedback should evaluate whether the message has been received, understood and has generated the desired response.

Communication may be spoken, written, or consist of overt or coded signals. The latter can be anything from simple smoke signals (still used by the Vatican to announce the appointment of a new Pontiff) to the complex and often subtle body language that we all use to reinforce our spoken words (from a quizzical raising of the eyebrow to shaking our fists). Table 4.1 shows the range of communication forms that are common within most organisations.

Table 4.1 Forms of communication

Skill	Form	Explanation
Writing	*Reports*	A formal report into an event or proposal.
	Memos (internal)	Inter-office communication is more often by e-mail nowadays; the memo has varying degrees of formality.
	Letters (external)	To suppliers, customers, advisers or other people outside the organisation. Usually formal and often can only be signed by more senior officers of the organisation.
	Note taking	Formal recording of a conversation, interview or a meeting. Circulation of a commentary/summary together with action points to others.
Verbal	*Speaking*	A natural part of our lives; the other side of listening, but how good are you at doing this clearly and concisely? Could you handle a telephone interview, for example?
Listening	*Comprehension*	Ability to understand what people are saying to you.
	Giving feedback	Confirming your understanding by summarising the other person's view(s) and taking action on that basis.
Non-verbal signals	*Body language*	Again, a natural part of human behaviour but one we should not take for granted. See below.
Presentations	*Structure*	Involves planning the message, its form, order and delivery.
	Use of visual aids	A picture is worth a thousand words but needs balance and control.
	Audience contact	Including your audience in your presentation. Reaching out to individuals with gestures and the use of eye contact.
	Handling questions	Finally, the ability to operate beyond your careful scripting and add further information/clarification to your slides.

Let's have a look at some of the skills mentioned in Table 4.1 in a bit more detail.

Written communication

Written communication is important since it allows us to communicate our thoughts very precisely, over distance and through time. Writing creates a permanent record that can be stored, filed, cross-referenced, duplicated, etc.

Text can be read selectively, if the reader is already familiar (or not concerned) with parts of the text. Lengthy reports will often contain an executive summary, which people will read before making a decision on whether the report is relevant to them and thus requires further reading. For example, the Managing Director may only wish to read the conclusions and recommendations for action, whereas others might wish to acquaint themselves with all the details of how and why the investigation was undertaken.

A word on Plain English   Sometimes, people who otherwise talk quite normally assume that they should revert to a stuffy Victorian style of English when they write. Sentences such as 'please be referred to your communication of the 14th instance' can more effectively be written as 'see your letter on the 14th'. You should always try to use what is called 'plain English', particularly if your audience is from a different cultural or linguistic background.

Plain English is defined as 'something that the intended audience can read, understand and act upon the first time they read it. Plain English takes into account design and layout as well as language.'

The Plain English campaign exists to promote the use of crystal-clear language against jargon, gobbledegook and other confusing language. It has an extremely good web site at www.plainenglish.co.uk.

Activity

The following examples of gobbledegook are reproduced from the Plain English site. See if you can rewrite them using plain English. (Suggested answers can be found on p. 93.)

1   High-quality learning environments are a necessary precondition for facilitation and enhancement of the ongoing learning process.

2   If there are any points on which you require explanation or further partriculars we shall be glad to furnish such additional details as may be required by telephone.

3   It is important that you shall read the notes, advice and information detailed opposite then complete the form overleaf (all sections) prior to its immediate return to the Council by way of the envelope provided. © Plain English Campaign 2004.

Formats and styles: reports, memos and notes   It is very important to appreciate to **whom** the report is being addressed and to understand their outlook and background. For example, an accountant must take care to explain technical terms to people outside the finance function. If you are writing to people higher up in the organisation, or outside it, the *style* you adopt in your language will tend to be more formal than it would otherwise be for, say, a close colleague or a subordinate.

In business, written communication takes different forms and styles, dependent on who exactly is being addressed and the context of the message. It includes:

Reports   Formal, usually high structured accounts of an investigation into something that has happened or a proposal to take some action.

Memos   Internal communication varying in formality and style. Could be a very formal message, say, from the Board of Directors to all employees or (at the opposite end of the spectrum) an e-mail to a colleague asking for some routine information.

Letters   External communication. Usually fairly formal in layout and style. Nowadays tends to be restricted to occasions of first contact or when a contractual position is being taken and the organisation's official stationery and an officer's signature is required.

Briefing notes Notes to formalise information: may be the discussions at a meeting or the concise summary of a situation (especially for senior managers who may not have the time or the need for all the detail and may need to refer to the main points in future meetings).

We shall now look at some examples, paying attention both to layout and style. (We shall leave letters at this stage as these will be covered later in the job-hunting section.)

Example: Report

To: Managing Director   Date: 4 January
From: Chief Accountant
Copy to Production Director

How can XYZ produce more effective reports?

Introduction

The external consultants have suggested that we improve the quality of our communication. This report examines the problem and suggests some solutions.

What is a report?

A report is usually a formal clearly structured document, often a lengthy summary of an investigation of a problem culminating in a conclusion and recommendation. Reports will use:

- itemised lists where appropriate (but with a sentence of explanation where necessary).
- diagrams
- Appendices

The problem

A number of past reports were analysed over 6 months.

Conclusion

Staff do not know how to write effective reports.

Recommendation

We should run some workshops on report writing next month.

Example: Memorandum

To: Site Supervisor   Date: 4 January
From: Accountant

Purpose of memos

These are documents for people within the organisation. Often shortened to 'Memos', they tend to be only a single page of paper, the purpose of which is to give instructions or to provide or request information. Nowadays, the memo is usually in the form of an e-mail:

Please pass this on to all your workers.
If I can be of further assistance please contact me on extension 1265.

Note: some organisations have standard formats, as do some training bodies such as the Royal Society of Arts (RSA). The format above is something of a generic one. You will find many variations in practice.

Example: Briefing notes for Chief Accountant's presentation

Subject: All about briefing notes

Purpose – gives information to someone in a form that can be referred to in a meeting or during a presentation
Preparation – intended to be prepared quickly and easily in a form that can be referred to whilst talking or presenting
Length – usually short; conveys key facts/concepts only
Style – bare minimum of words and punctuation

You should now understand that good communication is about understanding the needs and background of the recipient and presenting information in a form that is appropriate to those needs, the context of the situation and the objectives that you wish to achieve.

The importance of good grammar   The following list reports some of the most common grammatical errors found in student CVs, application forms and letters. For further advice on some of the finer points of the English language, see www.dictionary.com.

Whilst there are some people that hold the opinion that grammar doesn't matter in education as long as the sense of the passage is clear, there is little excuse for poor grammar in these days of computerised checking facilities. However, don't accept everything suggested by the machine, particularly considering the American origin of such tools.

It is easy to think that in these days of e-mail and telephone communication carefully considered English is not necessary. However, the increasing use of the world wide web for dissemination of corporate information requires great care, particularly when customers will be reading it. There was a time when the publication of any information to the outside world involved costly printing processes, and professional proof-reading was a necessary part of this process. Nowadays, web pages are updated quickly and continually and this needs constant vigilance regarding accuracy, presentation and English usage, otherwise customers will form a bad impression.

Get into good habits now! It will help you when applying for jobs in the future. It was interesting that in the analysis of competences gained and improved few students mentioned improving their written communication as an objective or achievement, other than in the context of using word processors.

Common grammatical errors in business and job applications   Just to reinforce the importance of correct usage of English at work, and especially in job applications, listed below are a few of the common errors that crop up in CVs and placement assignments:

- *Principal* – the first in importance, or boss, or sum of money, etc. *Principle* – a standard, or rule, or moral code.
- *XYZ Limited are a large company.* A company is a single body and 'is' should replace 'are'.
- Hyphenate joint words that combine to form a single item, e.g., the day-to-day chores, year-to-year, etc.
- *The circumstances of the client(s)* should be:
  - *client's circumstances* (if one client) or
  - *clients' circumstances* (if several clients)
- *'I speak to large amounts of people'* should be 'a large number of people'. Amount relates to quantities rather than a number of individuals.
- Most things in business are relative, not absolute, so use adjectives such as 'more' successful, or 'now tend to have a higher success rate'.
- *Practice* is a noun and *practise* is the verb; remember 'ice is a thing'. The same principle applies to 'licence' and 'license'.
- Spell out figures under 10 (e.g., one, two, three, four, etc.). It's all right once they become double digits and thus more significant in the text.
- Words in job titles tend to be capitalised when the position is being referred to, e.g., *'The Short Haul Manager is responsible for managing all the short haul flights.'*
- The *'company's directors'*, not the *'companies directors'*.
- Driving licence, not license!

Truncated words such as *admin.* can have a full stop (or period) to indicate something is missing.

Punctuation is a subject in itself and you would do well to brush up on the basic rules before writing application letters or starting work.

The use of English in application documentation will be discussed further in Chapter 6.

Listening: the neglected skill

Why should the ability to listen get a mention? We all do it from birth and if it was that important then surely there would be classes in it at school and university? In any case, listening in lectures and seminars has been the greater part of your life in education; why think about it now? Well, because employers want you to be able to absorb large amounts of verbal information and then be able to:

- make sense of it
- remember it
- and where necessary act upon it

Listening skills are especially important when dealing with customers/clients/patients, etc., when those customers may not be of your own age and background. Listening is a key part of our interaction with other human beings. You will need to show the interviewers that you can listen proactively.

It is never too late to start paying more attention to how you listen and trying to improve your ability to listen more effectively and show the other person that you are listening to them.

We shall discuss the importance of showing that you are listening in Chapter 7 on interview technique.

Remember: we have two ears and one mouth; sometimes it pays to use them in that ratio!

Body language: the use and interpretation of non-verbal communication signals

Body language consists of every part of communication that isn't spoken or written. Words make up just 7 per cent of the communicating we do, while the other 93 per cent comes from silent signals. Body language operates parallel to verbal language: the two are complementary, and sometimes contradictory, ways of communicating. Although it is common to dismiss people who gesticulate wildly when they talk as inarticulate, these people are, in fact, every bit as expressive as those who keep stock-still when they speak. Even those who have a good mastery of language, and think they've got their emotions in check, may not be keeping as silent as they like to believe when it comes to body language.

If we train ourselves to tune in to body language we'll understand what we really mean and what other people are trying to tell us. Sometimes our gestures just don't match our words. For instance, in a meeting a person may say they agree with you, whilst at the same time tilting their chair back and leaning away from you. By physically distancing themselves, they are actually expressing disagreement.

Sometimes circumstances make it essential for us to disguise our body language. Politicians who have to appear convincing, learn to use certain gestures to emphasise what they are saying and create the right impression. Some people are extremely good body-language liars. But the deceit may not be as complete as they hope, since the further you get from their face the more truthful they become. Feet and hands are a giveaway: Tapping feet and fingers indicate restlessness and a desire to escape. So much body talk happens at an unconscious level with signals beyond both our awareness and our control that we need to become conscious of them if we are to use them successfully.

Being aware of body language and decoding gestures helps us pick up other people's intentions, hold their attention and communicate better. Learn to recognise what other people's body language is telling you and respond accordingly. Body language consists of every part of communication that isn't spoken or written.

Communication is designed to convey a message and to generate a response or achieve an outcome. A simple statement, such as 'Close the door', is designed to achieve action (i.e., to shut the door).

The manner in which we say things, and the actions that our bodies make in delivering the message, will add further meaning or reinforce the message. For example, pointing to a particular door will help to define which door should be closed. Mock shivering might help to say why you wish the door closed; it may be cold/draughty. Moving towards the person slightly and whispering 'Close the door' might effectively be saying, 'This is a confidential subject. I trust you to keep this to yourself'.

We all use body language, whether we are aware of it or not. We all observe body language, often subconsciously, in others and we continually make judgements about people, their motives and any verbal messages.

Body language is especially important in the work place. These notes should help you to be an effective communicator both in sending and receiving information.

Examples of body language   The actions listed below are some of the key gestures in body language. Psychologists interpret these actions as meaning certain things. They may not all be true all the time, and you may be subconsciously scratching your leg rather than *hooking it around a chair for reassurance!* However, you will probably find most of them helpful at work or in your personal life to avoid giving the wrong impression of your own intentions and be better able to interpret other people's thoughts.

The Head

Lifted	Chin lifted to eye level of the other speaker. This expresses superiority, whether conscious or not. Also used when expressing insults or aggressive feelings.
Lowered	This indicates submission, acceptance, a feeling of inferiority, defeat or powerlessness.
Inclined to one side	A typically feminine posture that expresses tender feeling, understanding, comfort and support.

The Upper Body

Bent forward	A sign of involvement through curiosity or interest, or aggression if one foot is thrust out at the same time.
Slumped	Means tiredness, despondency or disappointment.
Leaning back	Indicates disinterest or nonchalance; a sign of distancing oneself from what is being said.

Legs and Feet

Hooked around chair	Signals a need for reassurance.
Crossed	Shows a desire to protect yourself; a sign of vulnerability.
Straight out	A sign of someone at ease.

Arms

Crossed behind back	A sign of shyness or a lack of confidence.
Crossed in front	Indicates suspicion, embarrassment or refusal to continue discussion.

Hands

Forefinger extended	A threatening sign.
Hands cupped	A desire to be precise.
Thumb and forefinger together	Means agreement or accord; spot on.
Clenched fist	The ultimate sign of resolution and determination.
Hand extended in a sweeping gesture	Indicates doubt, or disbelief of what is being said.
Palms extended outwards	An expression of rejection.

Palms extended inwards	A sign of welcome, comfort or sharing; wish for agreement.
Hands joined or crossed	A protective gesture when you feel threatened or vulnerable; need for security combined with the wish to disguise inner tension.
Holding a pen with both hands	A gesture of withdrawal that disguises nervousness and gives time to prepare for the unforeseen.

Activity

The next time you meet your friends observe their body language and try to copy their approach (with a degree of subtlety!). On other occasions act normally. Then ask yourself which meeting felt better. It's a technique that sales people often use and is called 'mirroring'.

Presentations

Public speaking, and particularly formal presentations, can be a terrifying experience for most people and even those people that do them all the time still get nervous before important presentations, especially when they are a part of a job interview. However, they shouldn't be seen as a daunting task but more of an opportunity for you to express your views, without interruptions, with your own script, with slides as prompts and with you being firmly in control of events. Sounds better already!

Presentations in various lengths and formats are a part of organisational life these days. It gives the chance to put your message directly to a captive audience; they may have filed your carefully crafted report in the bin but they have to listen to your presentation! But don't think a presentation is simply a talking version of a report – it is not! Presentations allow you to guide the listener through the important points as you see them and to bring the message alive. The way you speak, use body language, colour, slide animations or whatever can all add to, or detract from, your message.

You may be asked to make a formal presentation within the department whilst out on placement. However, many companies are expecting candidates to make a presentation as a part of the selection process. Whilst this may seem a little unfair for students seeking a placement it must be remembered that this is a competitive process and everyone is in the same position as yourself. It is unlikely that you will be asked to do a formal presentation without reasonable advance warning but as part of an Assessment Centre-style interview you might be asked to give feedback after a group problem-solving exercise.

If you are asked to make a presentation for interview then the following steps should help you structure your thoughts. Whilst out on placement one student was asked to prepare a 10-minute presentation on how to boil an egg using a PowerPoint-based data projection system. This seemingly simple task took the student about two days to prepare. However, she commented in her final report that the experience had been invaluable and that the audience of managers had been extremely supportive. This was her first presentation but she now felt confident about having to do other ones in the future. Twelve points for making good presentations are given below:

1 Golden rule: keep it simple stupid (KISS).
2 Introduce yourself and any colleagues.
3 State the objective(s) of the presentation clearly at the outset.
4 Give an overview of the rest of the presentation on one slide. Just like essays and reports, make sure that you have a clear beginning, middle and end.
5 Use diagrams and colour wherever possible.
6 Don't overcrowd slides and be especially careful with tables of data. Summarise the key points, or use handouts for the tedious stuff where necessary.
7 Building up information on slides is good but on the day it is easy to forget what is coming next.
8 Tailor your subject and style to your audience. Scientists might expect a different approach to the physics of egg boiling from, say, managers in the hotel and catering industry. Different folks, different approach!
9 Maintain eye contact with the whole audience. Don't use prompt cards. Take your cues from the slides.
10 Invite questions, even if you are praying there won't be any.
11 Use humour but avoid jokes!
12 Practise, practise, practise and don't be embarrassed about asking friends or family to be an audience.

Activity

Prepare a 10-minute presentation on a subject of your choice. If you'd like to e-mail the slides to the support site we'll put up names of the five best entries each month.

Working with and relating to others

Below is some information on this area:

Negotiation	Something we all started doing in the playground but at work we need to get to win–win situations, not grind our opponent into the ground! See Chapter 8.
Personal assertiveness	This is about respecting yourself and others, and it is a key part of being successful in the corporate jungle and at the same time enjoying it. See Chapter 8.
Dealing with customers/clients	Depending on your vocation/position this is a growing part of business life.
Handling queries	A part of all jobs; it is essential to demonstrate that you can listen, understand and then take the appropriate action.
Working as part of a team	A key theme of management these days. Putting successful teams together, working within them (or, indeed, leading them) is a skill that will be expected sooner rather than later.
Task management/supervision	A bit grand to label this as leadership but nevertheless you may be responsible for supervising tasks or even other people, some of whom may have worked there longer than you.

The ability to get on with and achieve objectives with other people cannot be overemphasised. Being a 'team player' will be a significant part of your career. There may well be a few exceptions to this, of course.

Much has been written about teams and you will almost certainly have been involved in teamwork already in school, university and various clubs and societies. Your employer is also likely to include you in various team-building activities. The important thing for an interview is to know that successful teams have clear objectives, positive leadership, mutual understanding and a mix of abilities, skills and roles within the team members.

A useful acronym is

Together Everyone Achieves More!

For further reading see the work of Belbin who suggests that effective teams are made up of individuals who play different roles (see www. belbin.com).

If at interview you are asked to undertake a task in a team you need to be aware of what roles others might adopt and what your preferred role is.

Whilst Belbin suggested that we all have a preferred role we can, and often do, assume other roles. If you see yourself as the ultimate leader you may want to change your position if it becomes clear that one or more other people also want to assume that particular role. It may not be in your best interests to fight a war of attrition with a competitor if both of you end up looking unsuitable for an employer that prides itself on harmonious team-working. Remember the comment from the first employer at the start of Chapter1. That company sets team-based scenarios which aim to identify applicants who can both lead and follow as appropriate.

Belbin's team roles (see Belbin 1981)

1	Plant	Advances new ideas and strategies, looking for different approaches to the problems in hand.
2	Resource Investigator	Explores and reports on ideas, developments and resources outside the group; creates external contacts that may be useful to the team; and conducts negotiations.
3	Co-ordinator	Controls the team's progress towards its objectives by making the best use of team resources; recognises where the team's strengths and weaknesses lie; and ensures the best use is made of each member's potential.
4	Shaper	Shapes the way in which the team effort is applied; directs attention generally to the setting of objectives and priorities; and seeks to impose some shape or pattern on group discussion and on the outcome of group activities.
5	Monitor Evaluator	Analyses problems, evaluating ideas and suggestions so that the team is better placed to take balanced decisions.
6	Team Worker	Supports members in their strengths, e.g., builds on suggestions, underpins members in their shortcomings, improves communications between members and fosters team spirit generally.
7	Implementer	Turns concepts and ideas into practical working procedures; carries out agreed plans systematically and efficiently.
8	Completer Finisher	Ensures the team is protected as far as possible from mistakes of both commission and

	omission; actively searches for aspects of work that need a more than usual degree of attention; and maintains a sense of urgency within the team.
9　Specialist	Feeds technical information into the group. Translates from general into technical terms. Contributes a professional viewpoint on the subject under discussion.

APPLICATION OF KNOWLEDGE AND NUMBER

Specialism versus generalism

If we focus on key specialisms and tasks at work then we can expect to be more efficient as our knowledge and competence increases. One of the main drivers behind the success of the Industrial Revolution in the UK, and then later throughout the world, was the principle of the division of labour. Adam Smith first advocated the idea that the smaller and more regularly repeated the task, then the higher the productivity in 1776 in his book, *The Wealth of Nations*. Henry Ford was perhaps the most famous industrialist to apply the principle to large-scale manufacturing at the Baton Rouge plant in Mississippi in the early part of the twentieth century.

One of the modern doctrines of business is about focus, or concentrating on what you are good at to create a competitive advantage. Some employers are looking for a clear and specific direction to your career and the skill set that you have. The phrase 'jack of all trades, master of none' has a lot of truth in it.

On the other hand, specialisation can be a trap. Mindsets and skill sets that are reluctant to change can easily become extinct. A natural tendency of human nature is to define physical and psychological territory and to stay within the comfortable boundaries that we have established.

The point of this section is to demonstrate that most employers want to hire people who can do both: that is, excel in their chosen discipline and at the same time see a much bigger picture where their specialist knowledge integrates with other disciplines and teams within the organisation. In other words, they have the ability to see linkages between theory and practice and between knowledge and application.

Obviously, the opportunities to do this at interview will depend on your individual discipline and the exact subjects that are being studied. However, it is a tricky area that can often floor applicants when questions such as the following are asked.

What aspects of your studies at university do you think will help in doing your job here at XYZ?
From your studies, what are the latest technologies or techniques that would help XYZ Ltd to make better or cheaper products?

Permutations of these questions are many and varied. The problem is that you have studied so much that it is often difficult to think of particular examples from your learning, but with practice it should be something that you can feel confident about. Make an effort to look through your programme content before writing your CV and preparing for interview. If you really can't see anything of relevance then talk to your subject tutors. Let's have a joke to illustrate the point about relevance, (apologies to any aspiring accountants).

Once upon a time there was man floating along in his hot air balloon, completely lost. He sees another man digging is garden. He calls down, 'Ahoy there! Where am I?'

The man stops digging his garden and looks up. 'You're in a balloon', he shouts back.

The balloonist responds, 'You must be an accountant.'

'How do you know that?' says the gardener.

'Because you're absolutely precise, but no use whatsoever to anyone else!' came the reply.

Exposure to other disciplines

Does your work experience cover other functions or disciplines? Will your placement allow you to sample life in other departments?

Number

There's a lot we could say about the importance of maths and number but we will keep things short as there are many specialist sources on the subject. However, what we do want to emphasise is that the ability to handle numbers is one of the key skills that employers seek and selection tests often include a section on arithmetic and/or basic mathematical concepts. Employers will also want to see that you can relate to numbers and put them into context. Again, don't neglect this aspect when preparing for interview; do some exercises and sharpen up. Think also about what numbers mean in organisations. Here's a daft example.

There was a tour guide who was showing some visitors around an underground cave system. He said, 'These caves are 32 million and 5 years old.'
The visitors were amazed. One of them said, 'How do you know the age so accurately?'
'That's easy', says the guide, 'I've been doing this job for 5 years and the caves were 32 million years old when I started!'

The guide's arithmetic cannot be faulted, but is he likely to make a good decision-maker in today's complex and fast moving environment?

INFORMATION AND COMMUNICATION TECHNOLOGY (ICT)

We really shouldn't have to say much about the importance of being literate in ICT. It is usually taken for granted that students in higher education will be highly literate in personal computing and be familiar with navigating the world wide web and using e-mail. However, precisely because competence in ICT is now taken for granted, being able to differentiate yourself from your peers is more essential.

Employers will want to ensure that you are indeed competent in the basic aspects but it is also worth making some effort to demonstrate that you have a progressive attitude. Show that you appreciate how ICT can be used by organisations to improve the way in which they work and specifically how your chosen company might use the Internet to market its products and share information with suppliers, customers and colleagues. You might also take the opportunity to create a web page to showcase your CV and expand some of the information. *Be careful, though, not to give any of the personal information that you would normally put on your CV that would enable someone to trace you.*

Examples of basic IT applications might include; wordprocessing, spreadsheets, MSPowerPoint, databases, e-mail systems, e-commerce, the Internet, and industry-specific applications such as accounting systems or market research packages.

There is a fine line between demonstrating that you are computer literate and switched on to the latest developments, and sounding simply obsessive about the technology itself.

Finally, don't ever be tempted to exaggerate your ICT prowess; a straightforward technical question can easily unravel the whole of an otherwise scrupulously honest CV.

References

Belbin, M.R. (1981) *Management Teams – Why They Succeed or Fail*, Butterworth Heinemann. www.belbin.com.

Ford, H., cited in Johnson, H.T. and Kaplan, R.S. (1987) *Relevance Lost: The Rise and Fall of Management Accounting*, Cambridge, MA: Harvard University Press.

Handy, C.B. (1990) *The Age of Unreason*. Boston, MA: Harvard Business School.

Shannon, C. and Weaver, W. (1949) *A Mathematical Model of Communication*, Urbana, IL: University of Illinois Press.

Smith, A. (1776) *An Inquiry into the Nature and Causes of the Wealth of Nations*, reprinted 1976, Oxford: Clarendon Press.

Woolland, A.G.B. (1995) 'Core Skills and the Idea of the Graduate', *Higher Education Quarterly*, Winter.

Further reading

Eastaway, R. and Wyndham, J. (2002) *How Long is a Piece of String?* Robson Books. 'More hidden mathematics of everday life'. Gives an insight into maths in a very readable manner.

Julius, E.H. (1992) *Rapid Math: Tricks and Tips*, New York: Wiley. '30 days to number power' is what is says. Over 2,000 problems to attempt.

Steil, L.K. and Summerfield, J. (1983) *Listening – It can Change your Life. A Handbook for Scientists and Engineers*, New York: Wiley.

Suggested answers to plain English activity

Children need good schools if they are to learn properly.

If you have any questions, please ring.

Please read the notes opposite before you fill in the form. Then send it back to us as soon as possible in the envelope provided.

Part II

Job searching, applications and interviews

5

Job searching

By the end of this chapter you should be able to:

- recognise personal goals, skills and values and match these with your career aspirations: what do I want to do?
- focus your research on appropriate sectors/employers/jobs: who do I want to work for?
- undertake a structured search of available opportunities: how do I go about getting the job I want?

GETTING STARTED: WHAT DO I WANT TO DO?

Understanding the past and predicting the future: 20/20 vision

In Chapter 1 we considered some of the changes that have taken place in the labour market, especially how these will affect people like you with your qualifications and experience starting a career. We might understand that working life is getting 'tougher but more interesting', but what does this mean for us as individuals? Clearly the changing nature of work in general is the context within which our lives and our careers, whatever we do, will be played out. We have already considered what has happened that has affected work and careers, but what about the future?

Activity

Either individually or with a group of colleagues, and with reference back to Chapter 1, list the main changes that have taken place in relation to work and careers in the last 20 years. You might like to think of changes that have affected your parents' generation and their work, or the geographical area where you have come from. What has happened internationally? What about PEST factors: political, economic, societal, and technological? Are there any demographic trends and issues we should be aware of that might impact on us later? If you are using this book as part of a taught course, why not present your ideas to your colleagues?

Now, try to brainstorm a list, possibly inspired by some of the things you have thought of already, which is of changes that will affect you in the *next* 20 years. If you are a typical undergraduate, this may well take you through to your early 40s, at which point you won't even be half-way through your career. That's especially so if the retirement age is raised to 70 (which might actually be one of the factors you have to consider). Again, if you are working through this book as part of a taught programme, it may be useful to work in groups on this and present your ideas back to the class. Don't discard your presentation, however, you'll need it later!

Think!

One of the things you might have discussed is the increasing power of information and communications technology. Try to think about the rate at which this has advanced during the period you have been considering. One way to find out about this is to ask people who have been in employment during the last 20 years. Technology is only one aspect of working life; others might include:

- professional knowledge specific to a particular area (purchasing, medicine, the law)
- personal skills; such as communications or delegation.
- organisation-specific knowledge; such as work procedures and operations in an employing organisation

The expression 'knowledge obsolescence', or the 'half-life of knowledge', refers to the rate at which knowledge goes out of date. Graduates and professionals are not immune to this and Chapter 9 includes guidance on Continuing Professional Development (CPD) to help you keep up to date.

Web resources

Try the following which include material on the changing graduate employment market:

- www.employment-studies.co.uk
- www.get.hobsons.com/career_guidance.html
- www.prospects.ac.uk

The on-line journal *Career Development International* also includes many excellent articles on the changing nature of graduate careers.

Back to basics

So, we have considered recent history, and tried to predict the future. But what are we going to do in that future? Starting the process of looking for a work placement, a job, or an internship needs careful planning to avoid wasting time and effort. Some individuals might have a very clear idea of what they want to do, as part of a long-term plan. Some students more or less have their choices made for them because the job requirements are closely linked to their course: examples might include agriculture, or pharmacy. For many individuals the choices are not so simple, so don't worry too much at this stage if you have no idea at all what you want to do. This section of the book starts with this assumption and some very basic self-analysis. If you have a fairly clear idea of what you are interested in you can probably skip some of this chapter and go straight on to applications and interview preparation. If your 'ideas' list is a complete blank at the moment, start here!

   In this section we will be working though some fairly simple self-analyses, some of which are included in the 'Sources and resources' section at the end of the chapter. The aim of the following section is to help you answer some very basic questions:

1   What am I interested in that I can turn into employment or experience?
2   What am I good at (skills) or what particular, perhaps even unique, knowledge do I have?
3   What do I dislike, and do I have options whereby I don't have to do these things?
4   What's going to be important in the future that matches with the first two of these statements (that is, my skills and interests)?

To begin to answer some of these questions let's start with an analysis of our individual strengths, weaknesses, opportunities and threats.

Activity: A personal SWOT analysis

SWOT is a technique that will probably be very familiar to readers who are business students, but it may be less familiar to others. It is not often applied at an individual level. First of all, working by yourself, identify your key

- Strengths
- Weaknesses
- Opportunities
- Threats

as you see them in your life and in your career. Try to do this completely on your own in the first instance because the answers must relate to you and you alone. You may wish to revisit Chapter 4 at this stage, which looked at your personal skills. While it's important to approach the SWOT analysis with as much of an open mind as possible, if you get stuck you might find the following suggestions useful.

Your *strengths* might include:

- your qualifications
- skills you have developed through hobbies or interests

Generally strengths are things that you have systematically worked on and developed over a long period of time, although they may relate to personal attributes such as stress resistance or a sense of humour (although these can be worked on as well!). You will have identified some of the skills in Chapters 3 and 4. In this chapter we will develop some of these ideas into a *self-knowledge database* (see below).

Your *weaknesses* might include:

- what you find difficult in your present course or in life generally
- problems with poor time management or meeting deadlines
- attributes that might hold you back (e.g., poor concentration, poor spelling)

Weaknesses are almost always things that you can do something about, and can often be remedied. This might be by training, by improving your study habits, or by identifying some specific problem and doing something about it. As an example it is often surprising to the author that students can go all the way through a school career and only be diagnosed as dyslexic when they reach university. How much easier would they have found their school studies with an earlier diagnosis and appropriate help? You'll find some information on dyslexia in the 'Sources and resources' section at the end of this chapter, or approach your student services or student counsellors for help and advice.

Opportunities are heavily influenced by your specific strengths and weaknesses but some examples might include:

- having qualifications and skills for which there is a high demand
- personal connections in a particular organisation, through family relationships or a part-time job
- particular events which might work in your favour such as a family relocation to another area
- being in the right place at the right time

If it sounds as though there is an element of luck in the above list then this is to some extent true, but opportunities can also be created by working on one's strengths and minimising the effect of weaknesses, which otherwise might be threats.

These *threats* in turn might include:

- adverse employment conditions (e.g., due to recession)
- an oversupply of people with your qualifications
- changes in the labour market due to technological change which mean your skills and knowledge become out of date
- family or personal circumstances, or health problems

While you can't control events in the external environment you can often influence your ability to deal with these, e.g., by strategically steering your career, sometimes referred to as 'career navigation'. You will find more on this in Chapter 9, which also covers how you can keep yourself up to date through CPD. For graduates, while the saturation of the labour market in many subject disciplines is a twenty-first century fact, it is something that can generally be overcome with a well-planned strategy such as self-marketing, which is covered in Chapter 6.

Below we give an example of a personal SWOT analysis.

Personal SWOT analysis: Amanda Jones

Strengths

Good 'A' level grades
My subject area suffers from undersupply: there aren't enough graduates (e.g., electronics)
Some prior work experience (part-time and vacation work)
Lots of CV-enhancing activities e.g., Duke of Edinburgh, charity work
Experience of teamwork and leadership both through extra-curricular activities (above), at school, and in the university sports teams
Multi-lingual (fluent in French)
Mobility – probably the key to future success

Weaknesses

Not very confident at making presentations
Very little interview experience
Can sometimes find it difficult to prioritise work over personal life
Tendency to take on too many things:
Find it difficult to keep skills up to date

Opportunities

High demand for my subject area
Work experience (post-school and through part-time work) in electronics assembly
Possible international opportunities through potential for overseas placement or employment

Threats

Depressed economy in my 'home' area
Too many commitments in later stages of degree, but still need to earn extra money
Possible recession in the electronics industry due to global events
Long-term challenge of keeping professional skills and knowledge up to date

---

When you have completed your personal SWOT analysis it is often a good idea to reflect on it with the assistance of a friend, a tutor or a colleague.

1 If they have done a personal SWOT analysis as well, compare notes. Is theirs very different? Why?
2 Does the other person agree with your self-assessment?
3 In the light of the discussion and your reflection, do you need to revisit your own lists of strengths, weaknesses, opportunities and threats?

You can now start to build up your *self-knowledge database*.

Identifying skills, strengths and development needs for a self-knowledge database

What exactly is a self-knowledge database? We need to understand what our skills, our strengths, our development needs, and our options are. We need also to recognise things that may threaten our ambitions. We can do this by building up as much information as possible about ourselves. In the database we can include:

- our reflections from the 20/20 vision exercise
- our reflections on the results of the personal SWOT analysis
- the results of any career diagnostic questionnaires we may complete, which are covered later in this chapter
- the use of Internet diagnostic materials
- our CVs (yes, there will be more than one, and these will be covered in Chapter 6)
- lists of potential organisations we can make applications to

Obviously the more information you have in here, the better!

Choices, choices

In this section we will start to use our reflections on what we have done so far to identify some possible career choices or, in the case of work experience, some likely fields of employment where we could potentially find the kind of development we are looking for. Let us now compare the three items that we have in our self-knowledge database so far. Through a subjective comparison we may well find that an appropriate field of employment presents itself quite easily. This will be something that integrates what you are good at (personal SWOT), what your aims and goals are (the work–life questionnaire) with changing trends and conditions in employment (20/20 vision). Here is an example.

(communicating + surfing/watersports)

+

(I'm not interested in working in an office/I live near the coast)

+

(expanding tourism industry)

=

working in sports adventure holidays or training

If you have a clear idea at this stage then that's great, and you may wish to skip the next section and go straight on to how to identify the organisations you will apply to. If you haven't, or if you'd like to double check to make sure, then the next section is about 'career diagnostics'.

Career diagnostics: choosing an occupational field

The first stop in seeking help to choose the occupational field to which you intend to apply should be your university or college careers service or career development centre. As well as having lots of useful information on available vacancies (which we will come to later), professional career counsellors should be able to help you:

- diagnose your aims and aspirations and make appropriate, informed, choices
- identify a range of opportunities in your chosen area
- identify resources that can help you

Career diagnostics and the internet

One of the main resource growth areas in this field in recent years has been the explosion in the use of the Internet for career-related information. As a gateway to a series of searchable databases it's a superb resource, although it needs to be used with caution: not all of the information is as useful as it at first appears.

There is, however, an amazing variety of career-related resources available on the Internet. Basically these break down into:

- things that are free and/or useful
- things that you have to pay for and/or are not useful

Many of the web sites will have diagnostic tools such as questionnaires that can help you identify suitable jobs and careers, although almost all of these are more focused on jobs for graduates or mid-career job-changers rather than people seeking a work experience placement or internship. Nonetheless, if you still can't decide on a suitable direction, or if your degree or other qualification is very general, and you have tried the counselling route, you might find some of these useful whatever you are looking for. The section below deals with career diagnostic web materials; on-line advertisements and applications are covered in the next chapter.

We have reviewed a lot of these web resources and include some recommendations here. Others, which are perhaps less generally applicable but may still be of value to some people, are listed at the end of the chapter under 'Sources and resources'.

Our suggestion is that you look at the 'free' and 'more useful' sites. Clearly when recommending students to web sites there is a risk that they can go out of date or become inaccessible. One of the criteria we have used in choosing these web sites was their accessibility and stability. If you find that web sites have disappeared or have become inaccessible then please let us know, and if you're the first to tell us we'll give you an acknowledgement in the next edition of the book! If decide to go it alone you should use a search engine with keywords such as:

- 'career choice'
- 'careers advice'
- 'career choices and preferences'
- 'career development and success'

You will then find yourself presented with a huge variety of resources, most of which are clearly commercial operations selling careers consulting services, books, tests, or other products and services. The fact that we've mentioned a site below is not an endorsement of these products and services; maybe we're cheapskates, but we think you should focus on the free stuff! Some are academic university departments, some are government offices. Many are specific to just one country, while others are more global in their ambitions. Again, if you like something new that's useful and not mentioned here, let us know.

So where do you start? Here are some recommendations, which we have tried and liked:

www.prospects.ac.uk

This one sets the standard for others to follow, both in terms of scope and quality of materials. It is focused on the UK undergraduate labour market and includes work experience-related links which we describe below. It has very comprehensive vacancy listings, but some of the best materials are the basic diagnostic tools: the 'Prospects Planner' will help you identify appropriate fields of employment by asking you to self-assess your:

- general skills
- people skills
- motivations
- interests

This will then identify relevant fields of employment based on your self-assessment, so is quite useful if you are at an early stage in the planning process. It has a helpful-looking link relating to work experience which takes you directly to:

www.work-experience.org

This is the site of the UK's National Council for Work Experience. This site focuses on employer and vacancy listings, which you can search by duration of placement (e.g., three months, a year), start date, geographical area, sector. The listings are very comprehensive and appear reasonably up to date. It also includes an alphabetical search by employer if you have a particular organisation in mind. Some vacancies are also listed by subject (e.g., law) but these tend to be the ones with very specific requirements. There's no diagnostic section so you need a pretty clear idea of what you are looking for. This isn't the liveliest site ever created but at least it focuses specifically on work experience, which very few others do, and it has fairly comprehensive coverage.

www.yini.org.uk

This web site aims to help students make the most of their year in industry.

www.yearoutgroup.org

This web site offers gap year information for those people who want a gap year but who don't want to leave the UK. Fear of flying perhaps?

www.doctorjob.com

This one offers 'graduate careers with attitude' (!) and includes lots of useful advice as well. Aimed at the graduate jobs market in the UK, it has a more 'fun' feel than the prospects site, probably takes itself a little less seriously, and as a commercial operation includes some cross-selling. The main weakness of the site is that it has nothing on work experience placements.

www.jobhuntersbible.com

This is a huge American resource based around the work of the best-selling author, Dick Bolles, who wrote 'What Color is your Parachute?' We've included it here rather than in the 'overseas' section simply because it's so good, although still very American in style. You have to try to ignore that and not use the same figures of speech in your own applications! The best part of this web site is the 'Career tests' section, and especially the 'Seven rules about taking career tests'. These are, for your information:

1   There is no one test that everyone loves.
2   There is no one test that always gives better results than others.
3   No test should necessarily be assumed to be accurate.
4   You should take several tests rather than just one.
5   Always let your intuition be your guide.
6   Don't let tests make you forget you are absolutely unique.
7   You are never finished with a test unless you have done some good hard thinking about yourself.

Source: www. Jobhuntersbible.com.

This is all really good advice, and the web site then leads you into several free tests that you can take. It also provides excellent links to lots of other resources. Some of these are:

- the Birkman Test: this is a 24-item forced choice (either/or) test
- various versions of John Holland's work, and John Holland's Self-Directed Search itself (this is reviewed separately below)

Overall the web site is fairly US-oriented but well worth looking at; it is one of the best sources of links to other sites we've found.

www.monster.co.uk

Monster is a huge web site which offers lots of links to other resources. We especially like the CareerStorm Map ('Where are you now – where are you going') which is about the goals you may wish to achieve in life, and the CareerStorm Compass which helps your analyse your values, skills, style and preferred subjects. Monster currently covers 22 countries, so there's a fair chance there's going to be something for you.

Recommended university web sites

Some of the UK's university careers advice centres have outstanding materials available, which can be accessed by students from other universities.

Again the following are recommendations; we are always happy to receive more!

www.derby.ac.uk/careers

This takes you straight to the University of Derby's excellent career development centre web site which leads you to lots of really useful information. This department has close links with 'Prospects'. Especially recommended are the following:

- career choice workout
- making your experience count (this one is really useful if you are about to undertake a period of work experience or an internship)

www.keele.ac.uk/depts/aa/Careers/workexperience/2wexp.htm

Another excellent site which is especially recommended for its links in the local area, some of which are run jointly with Staffordshire University and other Staffordshire organisations such as 'Staffordshire Graduate Link'.

Non-UK sites

Although these won't generally carry vacancy, work experience or internship information relevant to the UK, some of them have very good diagnostic sections. You may even like to think about working overseas (which we explore further in Chapter 10). Remember that some of the above sources (e.g., Monster) also apply to other countries but may have a separate site for each destination.

www.internjobs.com.

This site offers internships of various types and lengths to students. An internship normally relates to a longer work placement in a specific professional field.

www.jobweb.com

This is a US/Canadian site with lots of good links, principally to US/ Canadian University departments and resources, lots of information on career choices and resources.

www.projecttrust.com

Gap year information.

www.summerjobs.com

This site is about summer jobs (really!).

Resources that you have to pay for

There's so much information available on the Internet that finding out you have to pay for something is normally a pretty good reason for hitting the 'back' button. If you don't mind a small outlay then the following can give you some excellent insights, or just read around what they have to offer and avoid the bits you have to pay for!

www.assessment.com

This site is based on the 'Motivational Appraisal of Personal Potential' (MAPP) where you can complete a fairly long questionnaire; there are 71 items, but they are relatively easy. You will get an analysis result e-mailed to you. When you get you MAPP career analysis, it will cover:

- interest in job content
- people
- things
- and your 'top ten vocational areas'

The author's was a seven-page report, and was quite detailed and very interesting. This is an American web site, which really shows in the way the results are written (style of language, etc.) but it is genuinely informative and there are some good links to other resources.

www.self-directed-search.com

The Self-Directed Search (SDS) is an American career test developed by John Holland in the 1960s, and is probably one of the most widely used career tests in the world. This site contains lots of useful information about the SDS as well as the test itself, so it's worth looking at even if you don't take the test. If you do, it will cost you around $10.00. Like we said, it's up to you, there are lots of other free resources to use; some are included in this book.

And finally a book

An American text that makes for interesting reading, if not that relevant to UK job-seekers, is *The Complete Idiot's Guide to Finding Your Dream Job Online*, by Julia Cardis (Alpha Books, Indianapolis, 2000). Its limitations are that it refers to things, organisations and web sites that are mostly of concern only if you are job searching in the USA, but the general principles, such as advice on posting your CV on an on-line job bank (basically, don't, unless you are desperate), and lots of general material on job searching, make lively reading. A very comprehensive resource.

There are lots of resources on the internet to help you with career choices: we have space only for a few here. If you find something you especially like tell us (or tell us if you have any problems with the above).

It is very important that you keep a record of your Internet research and enter the results in your self-knowledge database.

ACTION PLANNING FOR WORK EXPERIENCE

Having decided on your chosen area, it is probably worth reflecting on *how* you want to gain the work experience:

1   Are the kind of experiences I am looking for normally available on a one year basis only?
2   Can I afford that? What are the financial implications?
3   Should I look for a summer placement or internship?
4   Will a voluntary organisation give me the experience I need?
5   Is the placement linked to an accredited module or part of my programme? Some universities (e.g., Derby) have 'Applied Studies' modules as a pathway on their combined subject (modular) degree schemes, whereas other placements carry no credit value at all towards your qualification; they are simply regarded as 'experience'.
6   Is there a mechanism for me to gain academic credit towards my course through part-time work experience or a part-time job, if I undertake a suitable work-based project approved by the college or university? (Some universities call this 'Applied Studies'.)

Almost any type of work experience will be beneficial, and will enhance the value of your Curriculum Vitae, and your own empoyability. The next section should help you focus on which organisations to apply to.

DECIDING WHICH ORGANISATIONS TO APPLY TO: ACTIVE RESEARCHING

Finding work experience vacancies can utilise three basic approaches:

- following up vacancies notified to the careers services or published in a series of nationally (in the UK) available guides
- speculative applications
- networking

Notified vacancies

These can be found in the following national vacancy guides, listed here in alphabetical order:

- *Focus on Work Experience* (Prospects/The National Council for Work Experience)
- *Guide to Work Experience* (GTI)
- *Placement and Vacation Work* (Hobson's)
- *The A-Z of Work Experience* (Arberry Pink)

Some of these also have supporting web-based materials.

Your careers service should also carry files of work experience vacancies, which will cover paid placements or internships, placement in voluntary organisations, local and national vacancies and overseas opportunities. The benefits of the various types of experience are discussed in Chapter 1.

Your careers service may also have some or all of the following reference books (here, in alphabetical order):

- *A year on, a year off*
- *Green Volunteers*
- *International Directory of Voluntary Work*
- *Internship USA*
- *Kibbutz Volunteer*
- *Summer Jobs Abroad*
- *Summer Jobs in Britain*
- *Summer Jobs USA*
- *Working in Ski Resorts*
- *Working on Cruise Ships*

There should also be publications tailored to particular subject specialisms, such as *Working in Tourism*, or guides to particular professions such as *The Hobson's Finance Guide* which include sections on work experience. Your careers service should have a range of specific resources relating to work experience in the legal professions.

Finalist vacancies can be found in the following publications:

1 *Prospects Directory* and *Hobson's Directory*: directories of graduate employers, outline of the types of vacancies employers are offering over the coming year and how to apply for them (also on the web).
2 *Prospects Finalist*: regularly published with updated vacancy information.

3 *Prospects Today*: national, weekly vacancy bulletin. Especially useful if you can start work straight away.

4 Subject-specific publications for finalists e.g., the *Hobson's Management Guide*.

5 Your careers service should also carry current editions of local and national newspapers. Make sure you are familiar with which days of the week specific occupations are advertising (e.g., *Guardian Education*: Tuesday).

6 Your university or college library may also carry specialist publications relating to certain professions or occupations (e.g., *People Management*, the twice-monthly publication of the Institute of Personnel and Development), although these will mostly carry vacancies for experienced practitioners.

7 There are also e-mail vacancy alert services, offered through www.doctorjob, prospects, as well as some profession-specific alerts such as through jobs.ac.uk for education related vacancies.

8 An increasing number of graduates elect to get into the organisation or the occupation they want by taking a lower level job initially, and then 'growing' either the job itself or their profile in the organisation. Graduate underemployment rather than unemployment is an attribute of the millennial labour market, but this is an increasingly popular way of getting entry to the chosen field; how you develop that opportunity is then up to you!

One option that is not as widely publicised as it should be is the Teaching Company Scheme, which is a partnership approach between a university and an employing organisation, normally in relation to specific technical skills and knowledge. Teaching Company Schemes are normally focused on high-quality graduates who are then known as TCS associates, who will work in companies, normally for two years, on projects which are jointly supervised by the company and the university. You don't have to do this in your own university (known as the 'knowledge base' in TCS terms) but this is the most common model. Generally acknowledged as an excellent step up on the career ladder. Worth finding out about.

Another excellent opportunity is the Shell Technology Enterprise Programme, which offers 8-week summer placements for penultimate year students (see Chapter 2).

There are also recruitment fairs held at universities around the UK, sometimes on a regional basis. Don't read too much into the fact that a specific employer isn't coming to *your* university. It is worthwhile checking beforehand which employers will be present: many fairs are typically made up of some professional organisations, selected local blue-chip companies, some smaller local companies and representatives of the voluntary or not-for-profit sector. Job centres are not often worth looking into for graduate employment, but may, like recruitment agencies, be useful for temporary work. Similarly, local newspapers will carry general vacancies, very few relevant to graduates, but can be a useful source of 'entry-level' jobs. Finally, your careers service should be notified of specific vacancies by selected employers, so it is important to keep in touch and check their bulletin boards regularly.

Speculative applications

There are a number of reasons why you may choose to apply for work experience, or indeed finalist vacancies, on a speculative basis. These include:

- you are interested in a very specific area of work for which there are few or no advertised vacancies
- you are interested in working in a specific geographical area or in specific organisations related to your interests
- you are interested in gaining work experience at a particular point of the year which is not traditionally catered for by more established provision

Whatever your reasons it is important to understand that making speculative applications is inherently less likely to succeed than applying for advertised vacancies, and the more limits that you put on yourself (geography, type of organisation) the greater the likelihood of rejection becomes. Generally, if there aren't specific reasons why you should go for a speculative approach it is best to concentrate your energies on either advertised vacancies or networking. Many organisations receive lots of speculative applications and don't necessarily read or acknowledge them: sometimes, especially for well-known organisations, there may be simply too many to deal with. There are, however, some advantages of the speculative approach, which are:

- if you do come across a vacancy, there will be less competition than for one that has been advertised nationally
- your commitment to the job and to the organisation should be higher if the vacancy relates to your specific and focused career aims
- using your initiative puts you in control of the process, which is fine so long as the high rate of rejections doesn't get you down!

If you are determined to try the speculative approach then the following resources should be useful, and most of these should be available from either your careers service or library:

- listings for final year vacancies (see above): at least you know that these employers employ graduates
- 'Kompass' and 'Key British Enterprises', which are directories of UK organisations
- there are some directories specific to certain types of organisation e.g., *The White Book* (production companies), *The Social Services Yearbook*, or *The City Contact*
- Association of Graduate Careers Advisory Services (AGCAS) Occupational Booklets (details of trade directories or journals)
- professional organisations such as those in accountancy will often carry listings of organisations which have regular traineeships
- hobby or enthusiast publications will often have advertisements for related organisations, e.g., *Practical Boat Owner* for yacht manufacturers and sail training schools
- your careers service will also have details of local employer directories or Chambers of Commerce

You can enhance the likelihood of success for speculative applications in the following ways:

1   Research the organisation carefully including product/services, current issues (are they in the news?), key people including the name of the person who deals with recruitment and their *correct* title.
2   Do a little homework by speaking to the receptionist (if there is one) or a member of the office staff: they should be able to tell you who does what, and some other information about the company.
3   Contact the key individuals by telephone to make yourself known to them: the personal approach takes a little nerve and needs handling with tact and care.
4   Remember that key people are busy people. What can you offer them that they should take time out to listen to you?
5   You may find that you get into a detailed conversation on the telephone which can become a telephone interview; be prepared for this and have some notes by you just in case.
6   If you do have a detailed conversation follow it up with a thank you letter even if the conversation didn't immediately lead to an interview.
7   Be prepared to visit the organisation and spend some time there; let them get to know you – you should be your own ambassador!
8   Even if you are unsuccessful ask them to keep your CV on file.

If you do get as far as a written application, ensure that it is not too long, and very quickly tells them what you can offer them that they might not already have. For small or medium organisations this is likely to be specific technical skills or knowledge, or significant achievements in a relevant interest area. If it is experience you want you may be prepared to consider unpaid work; don't offer this initially, but be prepared to accept it if you can if this is all that there is on offer and the experience is significant enough. This is a decision for yourself really, based on your priorities, circumstances, and the state of your student loan!

Networking

A much more efficient way of finding work experience, which has some attributes in common with the speculative approach, is networking. This means asking people you know, or with whom you have some connection, if they can help you make contacts in organisations that you can then follow up. Some useful approaches can include the following:

1   Brainstorm lists of everyone you can think of who may be able to help you. This may include:
    (a) relatives or family friends who may work in the industry or occupation you are interested in;
    (b) parents or relatives of your own friends and associates – do you know what they do? Find out; you may be surprised!
    (c) contacts through your recreational hobbies can be especially effective, where there is a shared interest: members of a sports club, contacts through Duke of Edinburgh, Scouting or a religious organisation;
    (d) contacts through entry-level vacancies (see above) can also be very useful;
    (e) often these contacts may give you access to further networks in a geographical area with which you are not familiar.
2   Use your own prior experience effectively, either through part-time work you have undertaken, or voluntary or community work.

Remember:

- that in some cultural contexts (typically in some Middle Eastern countries) personal networking is the most common way of getting a job, and that it is more common than you would think in the UK; what you are doing is not unusual!
- that you are asking for contacts not a job; it is your responsibility to follow this up

▦ to keep records of who you contacted, when, and what they told you
▦ and *always* thank anyone who gives you assistance

In common with the speculative approach, ensure that you research the relevant organisations carefully, and emphasise what you can offer them. Networking does not stop when you have found a job. Useful things to do for the future can include:

▦ keep the contact details for as many people as you can when you leave university or college and keep in touch; you never know when you might need them again!
▦ the motto 'do as you would be done by'. If you are asking for help, be prepared to help others in the future if they ask you!

Networking is an important part of professional and organisational life. Your future career may well be much enhanced by a professional reputation; work on it, and use professional or trade associations to develop your networks further. Some models of future careers see more and more individuals working outside organisations. To some extent this can be seen already with increased outsourcing in some occupations (e.g., training, some engineering specialisms, and human resources). Professional networks established now can help to secure your future in the long term.

It is also important to think about what you want to achieve through networking.

1 Do you want to evaluate your likelihood of getting a job in a particular organisation?
2 Do you want to identify gaps in your profile (skills, experience) that need to be filled?
3 Find out more about the job you want to go into by talking to some one who does it already.
4 Set up a work experience placement.
5 Set up a part-time job that will give you valuable work experience and be suitable as a short 'placement' in itself.
6 Establish a connection in an organisation you are interested in.

Whatever your strategy, the earlier you start the more vacancies you will have access to. If you leave the whole process until after your examinations you will miss many of the closing dates for advertised vacancies. You may also end up competing with the next lot of students going through the cycle!

SOURCES AND RESOURCES

The following isn't an exhaustive list but all the books, articles or web sites have been reviewed by the authors. We are always happy to receive new recommendations to be included in a later edition of the book. Similarly, if you find that any recommended web sites are no longer accessible please let us know!

On learning styles:

Kolb, D.A. (1995) *Organizational Behavior: An Experiential Approach*, 6th edn, Englewood Cliffs, NJ: Prentice Hall.

> This isn't an easy read and it isn't easy to navigate your way around the book either (there's no index), *but* it is one of the major works on learning styles.

> Recommended: pages 41–70 (learning styles)

For dyslexics:

www.iamdyslexic.com	Resource site aimed mainly at dyslexic school students
www.dyslexia-inst.org.uk	The UK Dyslexia Institute
www.bda-dyslexia.org.uk	The British Dyslexia Association

Other resources on work experience:

www.fledglings.net
www.prospects.ac.uk
ww.work-experience.org
www.qaa.ac.uk

This last is the web site of the UK's Quality Assurance Agency (QAA) for Higher Education. They have the job of ensuring that colleges and universities deliver programmes of appropriate quality. They have provided a lot of material on the rights and obligations of students, employers and educational institutions in relation to work experience. Worth looking at therefore to make sure that *your* college or university is giving you the support you deserve and are entitled to!

Also

Bolles, R.N. (1995), *What color is your parachute: a practical manual for job hunters and career changes*, Ten Speed Press, Berkeley, CA.

6

Job hunting I: getting to interview

By the end of this chapter you should understand:

- how to prepare your self-marketing campaign
- how to analyse job advertisements to recognise appropriate vacancies
- how to prepare a winning Curriculum Vitae
- the importance of first impressions: a high-quality covering letter
- how to present your case in an application form
- how to deal with on-line applications

INTRODUCTION

Having identified the type of work you are interested in getting experience of and the specific organisations you wish to apply to in Chapter 5, in this chapter we aim to help you deal with the early stages of the selection process: that is, from identifying the vacancy to getting to interview. This is a highly competitive process, and it is essential that you:

- are clear about your aims, interests and priorities
- show real commitment to the vacancy and the organisation you are applying to
- present yourself well in the written application, taking time and care over what you produce

This chapter will deal with each of the above learning objectives in turn, and ends with a range of recommended internet and other information resources to help you.

PRACTICAL STEPS IN 'SELF'-MARKETING

Although this book is about a lot more than 'how to get a job', securing employment is nevertheless probably one of the most important activities we undertake in the whole of our lives. Whether you are looking for a work experience placement or are using this book to help you find your first job after graduation, this chapter includes some advice and strategies to help you, and hints as to where to look for more.

One useful approach is to treat your job-seeking strategy as a marketing campaign with *you* as the product. Apply McCarthy's (1993) 'four Ps' here – to which we have added one (preparation) – in self and career terms.

PRODUCT – this is you! What are your attributes? They are contained in the self-knowledge database that you started in the last chapter – your values, your skills, your aptitudes – described by the results of career diagnostic questionnaires you have completed.

PRICE – what are you worth in the labour market? If you are looking for a work placement do you expect to be paid, and if so how much? What is the going rate (which means the normal salary) for people who do what you want to do? Would you be prepared to work for less to get a 'foot in the door' of an organisation you really want to work for? What is the minimum you would accept, and what is the maximum you can realistically command?

PLACE – what is your preferred job or placement location, and how flexible are you? If you are tied to a particular town or city or region, does this limit your choices? Are you aiming for a particular organisation or type of organisation?

PROMOTION – undertake market research to find information on jobs and organisations using the strategies described in the last chapter.

PREPARATION – write a 'selling' CV and prepare for job interviews, even if you aren't actually job seeking at the moment. You should *always* have a current CV. Guidance is given later in this chapter on how to prepare a CV. The web pages listed at the end of the chapter have lots of excellent information on writing CVs.

Activity

Using the first three of the Ps above, identify what you would put under each of the headings

Product – Price – Place

Think for a second!
    If you are unsuccessful in your first choice of type of job or organisation do you have a fall-back strategy?
    How can your networks (see Chapter 5) help you?

Web resources:

www.prospects.ac.uk
www.monster.co.uk
your university or college web site

MAKING WRITTEN APPLICATIONS

In this section we will cover the main ways of making a written application, by:

- CVs
- covering letters
- application forms
- letters of application

Curriculum Vitae

So far we have spent a good deal of time analysing ourselves and our interests, and trying to align these with jobs/occupations and specific organisations and vacancies. We've done enough introspection; let's get out there and start competing! If that sounds rather daunting, then it is worth remembering that in the jobs market, whether for work placements or longer term opportunities, there are winners and losers. If that all sounds a bit 'Darwinian' (meaning survival of the fittest), then yes, that is pretty accurate. What we should aim to do is to compete honestly and fairly (*never* lie in a CV or job application), but also to win, by presenting ourselves in the best possible way to the most appropriate opportunity.

So how do we write a 'selling' CV?

Remember that a prospective employer will probably know nothing about you other than what you communicate through the piece of paper sitting in front of them. It is therefore essential that it makes a good first impression, so a well presented document on good quality paper, well laid out and with a reasonable balance of conciseness and content, will create a very powerful first impression. We will consider content first, and layout later. An example of a possible CV layout is provided at the end of this chapter, but remember this is not the only possible style of presentation.

Content

Let's consider some of the essential details your CV should contain.

Heading   There's no need to use the words 'Curriculum Vitae' at the top: an employer will know this already!

Personal profile   In recent years there has been an increasing trend to begin a CV with a short statement presenting a brief overall profile of the individual. These need to tread a fine line between being too 'cheesy' and cringe-making, or being too egotistical and pompous. Used properly, they can be something that really makes your CV catch an employer's attention and turns a plain CV into a 'selling' CV. They should be no more than two sentences long, based on key words describing your qualifications, your skills and the main things you have to offer. Always write the profile in the third person, so it appears as if someone else is writing about you. For example:

> A well-motivated and flexible individual with excellent presentation skills, substantial experience of the retail environment, and an outstanding academic profile. Has demonstrated considerable initiative throughout her academic career in team work, voluntary and charity fund-raising activity, and as a student representative on the University's academic board.

In using a statement like this you are flagging up your main selling points at the top of the first page

Name   You should include your full, correct name as shown on your birth certificate. If you prefer to be known by another name you should state this.

Address   You should give your current postal address and also, if you live at another address out of term time or you are approaching the end of your studies and do not yet have a permanent address, another address where mail can be held for you, such as a family home. Be clear which address is which. You should also provide telephone and e-mail contacts. On these, if you have a voicemail, now is the time to remove any more 'personal' greetings. They may be amusing to a student colleague, less so to a prospective employer! If you have a personalised e-mail address, again now may be the time to think about what it says about you. One of the author's students (yes, you, 'Hacker'!) would sometimes find that his e-mail messages weren't opened because recipients were concerned they may contain viruses. Be warned! Don't give your student e-mail address: you will need one that can be accessed out of term time.

If you have a full driving licence, say so; and if it is 'clean', say so.

Date of birth   This is unlikely to be used in a discriminatory manner unless you are a mature student. Age discrimination *does* exist and there is no law against it in the UK. You may elect to leave this out but employers will probably assume you are hiding something!

Photographs are not traditionally enclosed with CVs in the UK. You may wish to consider whether the image could be used in a discriminatory way against you. In addition, what does it tell the employer about how well you could do a job? Very little or nothing.

Educational history   This is a bit of a balancing act. Too much detail seems like overkill, too little and the employer will wonder what you are hiding. If you are a student your qualifications are actually one of the principal features of the 'package' you have to offer, so you would normally go into a little more detail than, say, a more mature or mid-career job seeker. In the latter case one might question the relevance of qualifications taken perhaps 20 years ago. You should enter the names of your secondary school, and college or sixth form, with the main qualifications gained. 'Eight GCSEs including Mathematics and English Language at grade C or above' is normally enough detail for that stage. If you don't have those subjects at that grade or better it is likely to count against you, and you really should consider acquiring them at some point, or an equivalent. If you have particular skills even at GCSE level (e.g., languages) then state these. At 'A' level you should specify subjects and grades of E and above. For GNVQ or AVCE level you should give an indication of your general profile across the qualification (e.g., 'merit'). If you gained any specialist qualifications at school or college (e.g., an IT or languages certificate), then you should mention this, and also if you won any prizes for academic achievement at school or college.

Higher level qualifications, including your most recent from college or university, deserve more detail. Allow more space for the highest and most recent qualification. You need not list all subjects studied and grades attained, but provide enough detail so that the reader will have a pretty good idea of what you have covered. If you are a final year student or you know your overall grades, then include these. If your grades are not that impressive and you leave them out, then again an employer will probably wonder what you are hiding. If you have results pending or awaited, say so; *never* guess at what they might be. If this is the case and you have a 'live' application with results pending, as soon as you know what they are tell the employer. Remember that you may well be asked to explain the relevance of your qualification profile to your chosen vacancy at a later (interview) stage, or even to justify your choice of course of study.

Hobbies and interests   This is one of the most important parts of your CV because it says a great deal about what kind of person you are. Are you a team player, or a team leader? Do you take the initiative? Have you made the most of your time at college or university by participating in the life of the institution, through, for example, the Student Chamber of Commerce, sports teams or community activities? Beware, however, of giving the impression that you have spent all your time on your hobbies and too little on your studies. Consider carefully whether your interests may put off a particular employer. Also *never* lie or enhance your achievements to make your CV sound better. The author has sometimes been rather bemused by how many applicants claim to have represented their sport at county or national level. You never know, your interviewer may share your (claimed) sporting interests and know rather more than you expect!

Health would not normally be mentioned on a CV. If you are registered disabled there is no legal requirement to mention this on a CV (unlike application forms or an advertisement where it is specifically mentioned: see below), but if and when you are invited to interview it would be wise to mention it at that point especially if there may be access issues or you require particular support in the work place.

Referees need not be included on a CV. You may be asked to supply these at a later stage if you are invited to interview, and it is best to say they can be supplied on request. For academic references, you may ask one or more of your tutors if they would be prepared to act as a referee for you (normally your course leader or personal tutor if you have one). If you simply state which institution you attended then the reference request will be passed to the examinations department and then to the school or department and it may be some time, if ever, before it reaches someone prepared to write a reference for you. Better to specify a named individual, but ask them first and give them a copy of your CV. You may be asked to supply an employment reference if you have previous experience or a part-time job. References are a much more complicated area than they used to be, and many employer referees will only confirm basic details in writing for fear of litigation. If you are employed, do you want your present employer to know you are job seeking?

General guidelines

Do not use the same CV for every job. Try to customise your CV to meet the requirements of advertised jobs, or what you may find out about the priorities or interests of a particular employer. You should have one 'master copy' or 'long form' CV that lists all the things you have ever done in your academic or working career. This will almost certainly never be shown to an actual employer; it is a resource that you go to, to construct the CV that is tailor-made for a particular vacancy. As discussed further in the section on letters and application forms below, many undergraduates fall into the trap of giving employers the impression that they could be applying for any job with any organisation. Make your application focused and relevant. Try to identify the skills and qualities the employer is looking for in their advertisement and emphasise these in your CV.

Try to use positive words and statements. Angela Fagan's excellent book (see further reading at the end of the chapter) calls these 'power words', which may describe your character or your skills and achievements.

Try to ensure you-CV follows a logical order. If your list things in order (qualifications, experience) always use the same chronology, such as the order in which they happened (generally called chronological order). If you have used 'most recent first', say so. You may wish to use a fairly traditional order for your CV such as personal details, then education, experience, and finally hobbies and interests.

Pay attention to the layout of your CV. Try not to use more than two sides of A4, but leave reasonable margins (2.5cm is recommended), and left-justify the text, as it looks better than centred or blocked text unless you really know what you are doing. Never use a font size less than twelve points, and try to break up the sections with 'white space'. Use a clear font, nothing too funky, but try to avoid Times New Roman as it can look boring. Never use both sides of the sheet of paper. Never use graphics or clipart: they are superfluous. If you e-mail your CV will your careful design survive, or will it be lost in a different format on the recipient's computer?

Use high quality white paper (ideally 100gsm quality at least) and black print; do not be tempted by pretty colours as they may not photocopy well. Do not fold your CV; use an A4 sized envelope so that it arrives in perfect condition.

Check spelling and grammar carefully, then check it again. Then get someone else to check it. Do not rely on your computer's spellchecker or grammar check as it may not recognise certain words or grammatical errors. Never, ever, use text-language ('u'). Ideally ask someone involved in selection to proof read your CV and give you feedback.

Covering letters

If you are applying for work experience the letter that you send to a prospective employer is even more important than if you are responding to a job advertisement. You are asking an organisation to provide you with experience over a short period of time, with little prospect of a long-term payback for them on the training given, so you will need to use all your powers of persuasion to convince them that you *can* make a contribution and that they will benefit as well as you.

You must *always* accompany any application with a covering letter. It is, first, a matter of courtesy, and second, an important part of your 'selling' approach, to communicate to the employer what you can do for them rather than what they can do for you, and what makes you different to (and better than!) the other 60 or 70 letters and CVs that they have received that week!

So your covering letter needs to have instant appeal to the person whose desk it lands on. The initial impression it gives can make the difference between it being read, or an instant trip to the waste-bin. For this reason it is worth spending at least as much time on this as you do on the rest of your application. As with CVs, many students fall into the trap of using a general letter which could be for almost any job. You need to give the employer the impression that you are really interested in *this* job in *this* organisation, so do your homework! The following are some simple guidelines to help you. An example of a covering letter is provided at the end of this chapter.

General guidelines

Allow plenty of time to write the letter. If your course has deadlines for applications, don't leave it to the last minute or there will be no time for corrections or a re-draft

Always word process your letter and always use good quality A4 paper. Never send out a photocopied letter

Get the name of the person in the organisation who is responsible for selection or the area you are interested in and address it to them by name, normally by asking the receptionist or one of the office staff on the telephone. Get their correct name (with correct spelling!) and correct title.

Try to keep it down to one side of A4 if you can. The only times when you may vary this are if you are asked for a 'letter of application' which is dealt with separately below, or if the application form is very poorly designed and really didn't allow you to address the job requirements sufficiently. As general rule, keep it short and simple.

Lay the latter out as a formal business letter (an example is given at the end of this chapter). This means you should include the employer's address as well as your own, and a heading with the post reference number or title if it is a specific advertised vacancy.

For advertised vacancies, begin by introducing yourself and say what vacancy you are applying for, and where you saw it advertised. Then, in a few sentences, make clear and positive statements about how your skills, qualifications and experience mean that you will be able to perform effectively in the role. Increasingly employers want 'plug and play' candidates: people who can make a contribution quickly so that they can see a payback on their recruitment and training costs. In a placement, you stand to gain a great deal of useful experience, but what will the employer gain from having *you* on board? Describe the skills you have and how they were acquired, such as through team work or previous experience. Give some information about your course and how it relates to your placement, and what kind of placement you are looking for: is it a compulsory part of your course? Is it something you are arranging yourself perhaps during the summer period? Is it linked to a module on your course such as 'applied studies' (but don't use too much educational jargon)?

Show that you have done some research on the company by talking a little about the things they do, their products, recent (positive!) media coverage, or perhaps a training scheme they promote. This will help to deal with the 'general application' problem mentioned above, and personalise the letter to the employer. Don't set too many limitations such as limited availability for interview: there may well be plenty of candidates and the slightest problem can tip the scales against you. End by saying that you would welcome the opportunity to discuss your application further, and that you look forward to hearing from them.

Use 'yours sincerely' when you have written to a named person, *never* 'yours faithfully'. It is amazing how many students do this.

As with your CV, proof read it, proof read it again, and get someone else to look at it. Don't forget to sign the letter!

Speculative covering letters

As we said above, sending out s speculative letter for a work placement is a pretty high-risk approach so you need to make a very good impression. All the same guidelines apply as for covering letters except that in the initial paragraph you need to state very clearly what your interest in the organisation is, and really emphasise what you can offer them, otherwise there is no reason at all why the employer should take the time to read your application. It is best to send a speculative application to the Managing Director by name or some other named contact in the organisation. A couple of tactful telephone calls should establish who this is. It is best not to send speculative letters to personnel departments as they are more interested in dealing with specific vacancies, and it may be more relevant to send your speculative application to the head of the appropriate department. The difficulty with a speculative letter is that you don't have such a clear idea of what the employer is looking for or what their priorities are, although you can do some discreet homework either by telephoning the company, or by doing some research on their products, services and markets (which you should do anyway).

Networking covering letters

In this case you are writing to the organisation on the recommendation of someone else, so it is important to address the issue in the reader's mind of 'Who on earth is this and why are they writing to me?' as quickly as possible, such as in the following paragraph:

> I have been recommended to write to you by Mrs Sandra Wood, your Commercial Director, who is known to me through the Scouting Association. I am presently in the second year of a BSc (Hons) in Estate Management at Midshires University, and I am seeking a twelve-month work placement from August 200X. I believe I have the skills and knowledge to make a valuable contribution to the Redbrook Housing Association, which I will explain in more detail below. I also enclose my Curriculum Vitae.

As with the letters described above, it is important to write to a named individual. Because you are using someone else's name in your letter, it is essential that you seek their permission first *every* time you quote them in a letter (although some individuals may give you a more general 'permission'), otherwise it will be seen as an abuse of trust. Letters like these are much more likely to lead to a placement or even employment than a speculative letter because you have a 'way in' to the organisation, but do not be tempted to be too familiar. You should also assume that the reader, if they are interested, will ask your contact about you, so consider carefully what he or she is likely to say! The same guidelines as before apply to networking letters, although in addition you may wish to show it to your contact before you send it.

Application forms

Employers use application forms to help them deal with larger numbers of candidates in response to advertised vacancies. The form is used to 'screen' or select candidates who have presented the information in a standard format, which is much easier for the employer to process than large numbers of letters and CVs. Candidats who look promising will be invited to the next stage of the selction process and the rest will be rejected. It is important to understand the employer's agenda here: poorly presented application forms (in fact any poorly presented or scruffy application of any sort) will probably not be read and will simply be put to one side. Applicants who are rejected for any reason may or may not be sent a letter: sometimes the volume of applications received is so great that the cost of doing this would be too much. The form will follow the employer's agenda, and she will ask specific questions that will suit her particular needs (for example, financial services organisations will ask about your credit history). While forms help selectors make decisions, they are time-consuming to complete properly and you must allow yourself time to do this. The following section refers to traditional, written application forms, while the section after that deals with on-line applications.

Before you complete the form there are a number of things you must do. Photocopy it and then put the 'best' (original) copy in a folder until you need it. If you can make a second copy identical to the original (beware of coloured logos) then so much the better.

Read the job details carefully. There may or may not be a person specification (a list of the essential and desirable attributes the ideal candidate must possess), and/or a job description (a list of the main duties and responsibilities the post holder will be required to perform, organisational relationships, job grading and so on.). Try to understand the coded messages they contain: 'professional commitment' may mean a requirement to work long hours, for example.

Find out as much as you can about the organisation. There will almost certainly be a web site, there may well be annual reports, and it is worth using a search engine to check for media items to alert you to current events in relation to the organisation, possibly from the business pages or the *Financial Times*. Your careers service or library should carry publications such as Kompass which will provide company information, and there may be a relevant trade association or professional organisation in the case of, for example, banks or building societies.

Try to get some clues as to their culture (typically, 'the way we do things here', or the 'atmosphere' in the organisation), the management style, the employee relations climate, and norms of dress (uniforms?) and behaviour. You can then attempt to reflect these 'stylistic' values in your own application.

At this stage you should then think seriously about whether you really want to work for this organisation. Selection is a two-way process, and if you have found out that a potential employer has animal or human rights issues, are you comfortable with that? If you have read the job details and you feel that it is at best a 'long shot', then you are almost certainly wasting your time applying. If you feel comfortable with the organisation and you see a 'good fit' between your profile and what they are looking for, then go ahead.

Next, dig out your Curriculum Vitae, and applications you have completed recently. List the skills and experience (if they aren't listed elsewhere) that you can bring to the job and your personal strengths that you wish to 'headline'

Guidelines

If you hand-write the application, always use black ink (the form will almost certainly be photocopied) and 'print' your writing (even to the extent of using capitals) to a greater extent than you would normally, to help the reader. It is possible to complete application forms using a traditional typewriter if you are proficient enough but this is very time-consuming and employers in any case ofen prefer to see a handwritten form so that they can be confident you have filled it in yourself.

Use a copy of your 'long form' CV as a crib sheet to help you with the detail.

Neatness is essential. This can be hard to achieve if the form is written and your handwriting is normally poor, so make a copy of the form and practise filling it in. This will help you to see how the information should be laid out and whether you can answer in the detail the employer is looking for. Mature and well-qualified applicants can sometimes find a lack of space frustrating, so you will need to be sensible about how much detail to include.

Answer all the questions on the form in depth . This may sound obvious but some applicants leave gaps which is a missed opportunity to show yourself to your best advantage. The only reason not to answer a question is if it doesn't apply to you, in which case write 'not applicable' in the appropriate space.

Where you are asked to list things chronologically, such as courses you have studied, be aware that if there are apparent gaps then you will almost certainly be asked to explain these if you get to an interview.

If asked to identify the vacancy use the correct title, and the post number (if any), which will probably be given in the advertisement or on the job description. Large organisations may have many vacancies at one time; ensure you apply for the right one!

As with your CV, make sure that the contact details you give include an out of term time address and e-mail.

It is not necessary to list every single subject you have ever studied or every examination you have passed unless detail is specifically requested. You may, however, be asked to distinguish between education (school, college, university) and training (perhaps formal courses you have attended as part of a previous employment). Do not confuse the two.

If you are asked to provide details of previous employment it isn't necessary to list every newspaper round you had as a teenager; try to select part-time jobs which have some relevance to the post you are applying for, and highlight (as much as you can in just a few words) what you gained from the experience. Even the most mundane production job can teach you something about the nature of working in manufacturing processes: you may be managing one in the future!

Some application forms will ask specific, open questions, about (for example) your interest in the vacancy, while others will ask you for a statement of up to a side of A4 explaining your 'fit' to the vacancy. These are the most important sections of the application form, where the selector will be looking for clues as to your skills, your interest in the vacancy, and your level of motivation and engagement. Many candidates fail because they answer these inadequately.

If the job details include a person specification then you must ensure you state how you meet each of these in the 'free composition' sections. Then go on to ensure that you can perform all of the duties listed on the job description, if one is provided, although you will probably have covered most of this already in ticking-off the person specification headings. Fagan (2003: 109) recommends making two lists, one of the job requirements and then listing against these where your skills and achievements are relevant: this is good advice.

Take time over the 'free composition' sections, and allow time to revise if necessary. Ask someone to check the spelling and general 'readability' of your draft. It is a good idea to have a lined sheet of paper to put under the form when you fill in the 'best' copy to ensure that what you write sits squarely on the page.

Your activities and interests are very important as they will tell a prospective employer a great deal about what kind of person you are, and about personal qualities such as perseverance, team work, leadership, competitiveness, sociability, exercising responsibility and using your initiative.

Finally, take a photocopy of the completed form. It will be useful to refer to what you said if (no, think positive: when!) you get an interview. It will also be a useful 'crib sheet' to help you fill in future application forms.

Equal Opportunities Monitoring information is normally either at the end of the application form or on a separate document. This is not part of the selection process and is simply data that is gathered to enable the personnel department to ensure they provide a fair and non-discriminatory process.

Letters of application

Exceptionally, you may be asked to write what is called a 'letter of application'. This is longer than a covering letter and is the substantial part of your written application, replacing the CV and application form. The challenge is to make it 'fresh', relevant to the main points the prospective employer is looking for, while still being focused and reasonably concise. Below are some general guidelines:

1   Follow all the same rules as for covering letters in respect of format, presentation, and the use of 'yours sincerely'.
2   Do not use more than two sides of A4.
3   Do not use the same letter for every vacancy.
4   Structure the letter according to the broad job requirements as specified in the job description and person specification: try to identify which are the most important and deal with these first.
5   Begin with a positive statement that emphasises your interest in this specific job with this particular organisation (often a weak point in applications generally).

Example:

In this letter of application I will outline the reasons for my application for the one-year work experience post with Redbrook Card Services, identify those aspects of my experience and qualifications that are particularly relevant, and explain how I believe I can make a unique and valuable contribution to the Customer Services operation in the Newcastle Call Centre.

■   End with a summary statement of the contribution you expect to make in the future, and an indication of what you would like to happen.

Example:

I hope that this letter has demonstrated how my qualifications, experience and interests match your requirements for the post of Customer Services Consultant in the Newcastle Call Centre. I am seeking a challenging one-year placement opportunity that will enable me to make a valuable contribution to Redbrook Card Services, further develop my skills and knowledge in this area, and provide a foundation for my future research. I would welcome the opportunity to discuss my potential contribution in an interview in the near future, and look forward to hearing from you.

As with writing a CV or an application form statement, it is worth taking time and care to prepare lists of the things that you want to say about yourself as well as checking that you are able to address all the job requirements. If you can't, then the application may well be a 'long shot' and could be a waste of time.

How to deal with on-line applications

Before you even start to look into applying for a job on-line, you need to clean up your act in just the same way you would look to your personal presentation before a job interview. Set up a special e-mail account and choose a new e-mail 'handle'. Your 'waytoosexy41@ hotspot.com' may have been OK for use with your student friends, but it won't necessarily impress an employer. Think about how you present yourself in e-mail communications! Also a good idea at this time:

- tidy up your 'long form' CV
- revisit your key documents such as your progress file or personal development plan
- ensure that you are on track to get the grades you need
- visit your university or college career development centre, especially their web site, and look for any 'hot tips' or recommended links

As we identified in Chapter 5, there is a huge range of resources in relation to careers on the Internet. There are also many ways in which you can use the Internet in your job search: some are effective, some are not.

Less effective methods include randomly searching the Internet using one of the generic search engines. You are likely to spend a good deal of time looking at irrelevant material, again ending up with the 'spam' problem, and risk wasting time looking up resources which are out of date.

Posting your CV in a database is not very effective either. This really should carry a health warning, as you can find your CV may be widely distributed, possibly even to your present employer if you aren't a full-time student, and almost inevitably to a range of agencies who will keep on sending you spam until you change your e-mail address. The problem is, these aren't just for graduates. If you must use one of these databases, at least use one that is focused on jobs at the level you are looking. On the other hand, if you are desperate, or looking for any sort of exposure, go ahead! You can reduce the problems by:

- only posting your CV on well known, pass-word protected web sites (if in doubt check with your careers service)
- checking whether you control whether your CV is released to an employer
- removing your CV after you have landed a job
- using a CV that doesn't include your name
- *never* including the following on your CV: social security number, driving licence number, passport number, street address (stick to your *new* e-mail address: there's a world wide web of nutters out there: don't tell them where you live!), or reference information. You don't even need to put 'references available on request' as employers know this!

More effective methods include a more focused approach, as shown below:

1   Focus on specific organisations in your field of interest where you have already done some basic research. Research and review the web sites of companies you are interested in, and see whether there are current vacancies posted on these sites. Bookmark the sites and visit them regularly.
2   Visit the web sites of professional associations or on-line 'industry' magazines that cover topics and events in your chosen field. That way you will know what the current issues are in the sector, and have a chance to check the vacancy bulletins. You may even get involved with some of the discussion groups, and use this for personal networking.
3   Using some of the major online resources such as 'prospects', 'workexperience.org', 'fledglings.net', 'Hobson's.com', or 'graduate-careersonline'. Some of these carry links to specific vacancies; most are UK-specific; and many carry other resources and advice. Prospects also publishes a free e-mail newsletter ('e-prospects') which you can subscribe to, which incorporates a searchable database of job vacancies and training opportunities, including links to postgraduate study opportunities. This newsletter also provides links to temporary job vacancies, and there is a facility for a vacancy alert via e-mail or text message.

Use the Internet also for networking purposes. This can be through professional associations, newsgroups or discussion fora that you have an interest in.

So, assuming that you have negotiated the pitfalls of the Internet, and you have identified a job or placement vacancy in an organisation that you feel is right for you, what next?

Again, some words of caution:

1   *Do not* find the job of your dreams and instantly start filling in the application form on-line. Some of these 'time-out' if you are too slow filling them in. It is better to print the form off if you can, *then* make a copy of it, then have a go at filling it in, in a 'rough' format before moving to the word-perfect version. The standard rules on application forms (see above) apply.

2   You may be presented with an on-line psychometric assessment. Fill this in quickly and honestly, and do it yourself. There are actually some concerns in the human resources profession about on-line psychometrics, due to fears on the part of recruiters that they don't actually know if it is the candidate who filled the form in, if they aren't actually present! Never attempt to 'cheat' in a psychometric assessment. You are only cheating yourself. The same applies to so-called 'biodata' questions (e.g., when you were very young, with whom did you spend most of your play time?). While these may be pretty transparent (like the one here which is from a bank's application form; obviously they aren't looking for loners) it is best to answer as honestly as possible.

3   Remember that the reason recruiters use on-line methods is that they can get access to a huge number of potential candidates very quickly. This means that there is a lot of competition.

Here are some basic things that you can do to enhance your chances of success in on-line applications:

1   Keep a record of your applications and make a note in your diary one month ahead to check progress.
2   Update the 'long form' of your CV and be prepared to cut and paste from this to tailor it to different vacancies.
3   Revisit your transferable skills: if you have a progress file or personal development portfolio, make sure it is up to date.
4   Because some on-line application processes screen CVs by keywords, develop a list of keywords that will 'hit the right buttons' with selectors.

These may include:

(a)   team player;
(b)   persistence;
(c)   determination;
(d)   well organised;

(e)   presentation skills;
(f)   adaptable;
(g)   proactive;

and so on. Get the general idea? These keywords can also appear in an on-line covering letter, which may be scanned rather than read, so again, hit the right buttons. Read some of the employer's literature, and see if you can spot what they are looking for.

APPLYING FOR JOBS

So far we have principally focused on applying for short periods of work experience, perhaps up to one year in duration. While this isn't specifically a 'how to get a job' book (see below for some recommendations), much of the guidance here will also apply to more permanent positions, with the following key differences:

1   Remember to emphasise how the post you are applying for fits in with your long-term career plan. Your first job on graduation may well not be what was traditionally understood as a 'graduate level' job. Increasingly graduates will focus on getting into their employer of choice, then 'growing the job' or developing their own profile, within their chosen field.

2   If you are applying for a 'graduate level' job, remember to emphasise how you see yourself making a longer-term commitment to this organisation than just a twelve-month period. Graduate recruitment is expensive, and as we identified in Chapter 1 employers are looking for graduates who can 'hit the ground running' and repay that investment. Graduates often regard their first substantial post as a stepping stone to other things and, even if it is, an employer will not be impressed if you give the impression they are simply a means to an end.

3   It is also important to identify how you may see your career developing in the future, including your CPD, discussed in more detail later in the book. This will help to convince the employer that you are serious about, and dedicated to, your personal and professional development, as well as committed to the organisation.

CONCLUSION

This chapter has attempted to deal with the practical aspects of getting a work placement, much of which is also applicable to getting a longer-term job at the end of your studies. Before moving on, let's just take stock of what has been considered so far in this book:

1 The early chapters emphasised the importance and 'added value' achieved through work-based learning, especially work placements, and why this is especially important in today's labour market.
2 The range of potential opportunities was considered, including the 'traditional' 9–12 month placement, project or short-term work, voluntary work, and working overseas.
3 We have considered the importance of skills development, assertiveness and communications.
4 And in the last chapter, we considered ways of identifying what you are interested in so that you can make a more focused job search informed by an understanding of your abilities, goals and aspirations.
5 Finally, in the present chapter we have considered a range of application strategies and how these can be tailored for different situations.

The next chapter takes us beyond the early stages of the recruitment process to dealing with the main selection processes commonly utilised in recruitment for work placement and graduate positions.

CV example

David Clarke

Term address:	**Home address:**
22 Garden Terrace	13 Hemlock Close
Mainville	Bolton
MZ22 3EU	BL9 9RT

Mobile: 07765266246
E-mail: dclarky999@hotmail.com
Date of birth: 10.10.80
Nationality: British

EDUCATION

2003 Midshires University BA (Hons) Marketing
2nd year modules 2002–2003:

Business Research Methods	Customer Insights
Marketing Communications	Sales Management
Public Relations	Service Focused Marketing
Marketing Research Methods	Business Analysis and Systems Development

1st year modules 2001–2002:

Quantitative Analysis	Accounting For Business
Organisational Behaviour	Business Law

Information Technology	Business Economics
Marketing Fundamentals	Marketing Awareness

Skills developed from degree

- The increased emphasis on teamwork through group projects has illustrated to me the importance of teamwork while improving my group skills.
- The increase in independence, with being a student, means that I have learnt how to manage my time in completing my assignments while living as a student.
- My IT skills have improved greatly after completing a module in the subject area, which involved Microsoft Word and Excel.
- As well as the above I have also gained enhanced skills in research methods and presentation skills.

EDUCATION CONTINUED

1992–1999 The Lowlands School
A level: English Literature (C), History (D), Business Studies (A)
GCSE: 2×B, 5×C, 2×D, including English and Maths.

EMPLOYMENT

Summer 2001 Anglian Fabrics (through the employment agency Workforce)

- Responsible for stock taking, which involved me having to work reliably and independently.

1999–2001 Tesco Stores

- Developed my interpersonal skills.
- Reliable in dealing with tills.
- Competent team member.
- Learnt the importance of work delegation.
- Successfully adapted to different roles at short notice.

INTERESTS & ACTIVITIES

University

- An active member of University five-a-side football team, playing matches twice a week.
- Member of the University tennis club.
- I regularly attend the local gym to keep myself fit.
- I enjoy socialising and meeting new people.

Sixth Form

- A member of the college eleven-a-side football team and tennis club.
- Participated in the 'old poets, young poets' competition, in which I reached the final stage, requiring me to recite my work at the town hall.
- An enthusiastic member of the scouting movement.

REFEREES

Mrs L. Robinson	Mr B. Potter
Head Teacher	Human Resources Manager
Lowlands School	Tesco Stores Ltd.
Bolton	Bolton
BL88 6PQ	BL99 7RF

Examples of covering letters

The following is an example of a 'first attempt' at a covering letter for a work placement vacancy. An amended (and improved!) version is provided below.

Dear Mr Bird

REF: UNDERGRADUATE WORK PLACEMENT

I am writing to apply for the student placement position advertised on the Midshires University website. At present I am an enthusiastic second year student studying BA (HONS) Marketing at Midshires University and am keen to complete a year's placement.

The degree course I am following contains modules on Marketing Research, Marketing Communications, Public Relations, IT and Customer Insights. All of which I believe these would be the attributes required for the position you are seeking to fulfil. I am very much a people person and have the drive and ambition to make a difference.

I am keen to put what I have learnt into a practical situation in a business of your context and would appreciate the opportunity to meet with you to discuss the placement in more detail. I have now returned home for the summer vacation but would be available for an interview at a time to suit you.

Yours faithfully
David Clarke

Activity

Identify the shortcomings of this letter. Why do you think it might be rejected by a prospective employer?

Updated version of covering letter

Dear Mr Bird

Placement Vacancy

I wish to apply for the student placement position advertised on the Midshires University website. I am an enthusiastic, hard working student and have just completed the second year of study for BA (Hons) Marketing within The Midshires Business School at Midshires University. A requirement of this programme is to complete a period of work-related learning in industry.

Having studied your advertisement, I anticipate that the position would require a confident, competent person with an excellent grounding in marketing and business studies. The knowledge that I have acquired on this very demanding degree programme covers a range of subjects from fundamental market research and product design to marketing communication strategies. The programme also contains general business-related modules such as accounting, organisational behaviour, law and, perhaps most importantly, the practice and theory of Information Technology.

University life has also added to my previous work experience by helping me to develop my interpersonal skills, particularly the ability to relate to other people and to work as a member of team in pressurised situations.

I believe that I can make a contribution to AES and would welcome the opportunity to further explain to you how I might apply my existing knowledge and continue to learn and develop within your company.

You may already be aware of the Business School's Guide for work Experience Providers and further information on how students can work in business is available at http://midshirescareers.ac.uk/placements.asp.

I look forward to hearing from you.

Yours sincerely

David Clarke

Commentary

So why is the new, updated version an improvement? Here are some suggestions, although you may have other ideas of your own!

1　'I am writing'…yes, of course you are, David!
2　In the 'new' first paragraph, David has told the employer a little about the University and why he is applying for a placement.
3　The second paragraph reinforces the impression that David is really interested in that particular vacancy, and adds some detail as to what his course has included.
4　The statement 'I am…a people person' in the first letter is guaranteed to make any reader cringe! Much better, as in the updated version, to emphasise some of the things he has gained from university life in addition to academic study, which he has expanded on in his CV.
5　The updated letter also emphasises the contribution he can make (a 'selling' approach) as opposed to what he aims to get out of the placement ('gimme, gimme'!), while still emphasising his long-term development.
6　Finally David has provided an opportunity, through quoting one of his University's web resources, for the employer to find out more later, without overloading them with information at this time.
7　And finally…Yours sincerely!

Example of a speculative letter

Although this can be a high-risk approach, sometimes a speculative letter, as described earlier in the chapter, may be appropriate. This is an example of one that has been successfully used by a placement student.

Dear Mr Marchant

REF: UNDERGRADUATE WORK PLACEMENT

At present I am an enthusiastic second-year student studying BA (Hons) Marketing at Midshires University and am keen to complete a year's placement commencing 2004. If your company does not offer a placement I could be employed to aid with any special projects the company requires to be undertaken or perhaps fill any junior management position that has become temporarily vacant.

Since studying Business Studies at A-Level I have become more and more interested in marketing and so decided to continue with the topic to degree level. I would therefore be particularly interested in the area of Marketing but be equally as keen to be employed on a more general level, which would enable me to develop my business skills to our mutual benefit.

I would welcome the opportunity to work in the office sector of the market where I believe there is a tremendous opportunity to interface with new and existing customers through e-commerce. I enjoy working and dealing with the people and am adaptable to new situations. I am also competent at working in team situations and on my own initiative. I am eager to apply what I have learnt into practical situations in a business of your context.

Enclosed is my CV; however, I would very much appreciate the chance to meet you in person to discuss any possibilities regarding a placement. I look forward to hearing from you.

Yours sincerely

Checklist/self-assessment form: CVs, covering letters and application forms
Use the information below as a final check on your CV, applicaation forms and covering letters.
All documents

1   Is spelling and grammar PERFECT?

    (a)   checked by you
    (b)   computer spell and grammar checker used
    (c)   checked by a friend

2   Do the three documents:

    (a)   maintain consistency throughout?
    (b)   develop different aspects as appropriate; are they tailored to the information required of each one?

3   Does the package look forwards as well as backwards?
4   Have the application requirements been met?

    (a)   all forms included
    (b)   references up to date, with current contact details
    (c)   covering letter signed (with Yours faithfully or sincerely, as appropriate)
    (d)   documents secured together
    (e)   closing date met

5   Have you undertaken a skills/experience audit of yourself against the job description? Why do you believe that *you* can do this job?
6   Is the style proactive or passive?

CV

1   Does your CV make an impression?

    (a)   presentation
    (b)   length (two full sides of A4 where possible)
    (c)   information easy to find

2   Are the dates continuous and accurate?
3   Is all relevant experience included?
4   Would you employ you, based on your CV?
5   Has a friend checked it?
6   Have you compared it to other CVs?

Covering letter

1   Have you introduced yourself, your programme of study and the placement year concept?
2   Have you told them when you will be available for work and for how long?
3   If you are replying to an advertisement, is it clear which job you are applying for?
4   Does your letter bring out the skills/talents you can offer (refers to your CV but doesn't repeat it)? If you were an employer, would it make you want to read your CV?
5   Have you mentioned why this company/position appeals to you? Does this paragraph show you have done some research on the company?
6   Have you thanked them for considering your application?
7   Is the salutation correct? Do you know the difference between Yours sincerely and Yours faithfully?

Application form

1   Have you taken a copy/downloaded the form to practise on before tackling the real thing?
2   Have you read the instructions thoroughly before you start, particularly sections with multiple choice answers?
3   Have you used different examples of skills/experience in each section in order to maximise information/impression given?
4   Are your answers positive? Have you eliminated all negatives?
5   Is your handwriting neat and legible? If you were shortlisting scores of applications, would you take the time to decipher the writing, or would you discard your application as too time-consuming to bother with?
6   Are there any sections required to be completed by a member of academic staff?
7   If you have a disability, have you asked for guidance on completing the equal opportunities section?
8   Have you signed and dated the form?
9   Have you included all documentation requested?

Reference

McCarthy E.J. (1993), *Basic marketing: a global-managerial approach*, 11th edn, Honewood, Illinois: Irwin.

Further reading

Applying for jobs

Prospects Directory and www. prospects.ac.uk: this book should be available in your university or college careers centre, and includes excellent information on the world of work, job seeking, and making applications.

As an overall guide: *Brilliant Job Hunter's Manual* by Angela Fagan (2003) London: Pearson Professional Education.

Although not specifically aimed at university or college students this is a very comprehensive book that covers all stages of the selection process.

Hobson's career guides are aimed at specific fields but also include good general information on how to make job applications.

Before you apply: *Rate Yourself! Assess your skills, personality and abilities for the job you want,* by Marthe Sansregret and Dyane Adams (1998) Lata: Kogon Page.

This book helps to find your strengths and weaknesses; what skills do you possess which make you employable? This guide provides checklists that enable you to assess your abilities in all areas, including: communication, interpersonal skills and problem-solving. There are self-assessment quizzes to identify skills and weak areas, which you can then work on improving.

Writing CVs: *How to write a winning CV* by Alan Jones (2001), London: Arrow (Random House).

Examines in detail every section of the CV, providing real-life examples of CVs that worked, as well as some that didn't.

Covering letters: *Readymade Job Search Letters* all the letters you need for a successful, as by Lynn Williams (2000), London: Kogan Page.

Contains a wide selection of letters that can be adapted for your own use. As well as advice, examples of sample letters to cover a variety of situations: covering letters to accompany CVs and application forms, speculative letters, letters to ask for an introduction and letters to answer advertised vacancies. There is also material on e-mail job hunting and using the Internet as a search tool.

The Internet: *The Complete Idiot's Guide to Finding Your Dream Job Online* by Julia Cardis (2000), Indianapolis: (Macmillan USA).

The American text contains many useful hints for searching the Internet, but has the downside that many of the recommended references are US-specific. However, as a general guide to searching on and applying through the Internet, it has some value. Useful sections on web etiquette, networking and some of the dangers of broadcasting your CV too widely.

7

Job hunting II: interviews and other opportunities to shine

By the end of this chapter you should understand:

- the different requirements of the main types of interview
- how to prepare for interview: interview image and presentation
- how to conduct oneself effectively in an interview situation
- how to utilise effective question and answer techniques
- how to deal with assessment centres
- how to deal with psychometric tests

INTRODUCTION

In the previous chapter we looked at a range of strategies to bring your application to an employer's attention, and ideally to the point at which you might be invited to the next stage of the selection process. This chapter aims to provide you with the information you need so that you can prepare for interviews, psychometric tests and other selection methods, and what to do when these are combined in an assessment centre (more on these below).

This chapter is therefore written with the assumptions that you have diagnosed your area of work interest, that you have identified your employers of choice, and that your self-marketing strategy worked to the extent that your written application has been successful. Now you have the chance to 'close the deal' and get the job you want!

PREPARING FOR THE NEXT STAGE OF THE SELECTION PROCESS

Interviews

Congratulations! Your 'selling' exercise has worked and you have been invited to interview. But what sort of interview is it? There are a number of different types and it is worthwhile considering this before you start to prepare for the interview itself. In general, remember the following points:

1   An interview is a 'conversation with a purpose'. No matter how chatty or friendly the interviewer or interviewers may seem, remember that they are there to do a job, which is to decide whether you are the best person for their job or placement opportunity. Your task is to convince them of this!

2   Unless you have got to the interview through a strong personal network the person or people interviewing you know nothing about you other than what you have communicated by your CV, your application form and covering letter and, of course, by how you physically present yourself to them! Presentation, posture and body language suddenly become very important and are discussed in more detail below.

3   An interview is a two-way process. No matter how much you may have wanted to work for this organisation in the past, or to do a particular job, you need to decide whether this job, in this organisation, really is what you want. What is the culture and 'climate' of the organisation? What are the tasks that you will actually be doing? Who will you be working with? Where will you be working? Will you be working in one location, or travelling around? What training will you receive? Will the organisation (if this is a job, not a placement vacancy) support your continuing professional development (CPD), possibly towards a professional qualification? If you feel that you aren't getting the answers to these concerns from any other source (e.g., you may have a presentation), then it is your responsibility to check these out yourself by asking questions. Some sample questions are listed later in the chapter. If you feel that there are too many 'no' answers to your questions, then this may not be the job for you. After all, you don't have to accept it, and if you feel uncomfortable with some aspects of the organisation then it may be best to withdraw as a damage limitation strategy.

4 Even though interviews have a relatively poor ability to predict whether or not an appointment will be successful, are not that efficient at picking the best person for the job, and are time consuming and expensive, almost all employers use them, so you had better learn how to deal with them

While this book is written from the student's point of view, Human Resource managers in organisations have a duty to ensure that recruitment and selection are conducted fairly and properly. This means that employers should:

- work within the law and not ask questions related to race, sex or disability
- ask all the candidates more or less the same questions, with some flexibility for 'probing' (asking more detailed questions, perhaps to follow up a point that needs clarification)
- train their interviewers in appropriate interview styles, and ensure they have a working knowledge of the relevant employment law
- have a person specification that clearly communicates the skills required in this job, so that you can be assessed against these in the interview
- be prepared to give feedback after the interview. If this is not offered, and you have received a decision one way or the other, then you should telephone the following day to ask for feedback. Many individuals forget to seek feedback if the appointment has been successful, but it is good to know what you have done right!

In the chapter heading we described an interview as an 'opportunity to shine'. This is absolutely true. An interview should be seen as an opportunity to give a good account of yourself, to present your skills and attributes honestly but positively, to showcase your achievements and the positive attributes you have developed and the experiences you have gained while studying.

Types of interview

Before we consider some of the more detailed aspects of interpersonal interactions during interviews, let us first consider the various sorts of interview we might encounter.

Preselection interviews are used by employers who may have a multi-stage selection procedure. The aim of this stage is to ascertain your general suitability before a more detailed assessment is undertaken. If you are applying to a national organisation such as a bank or a retail chain, then the preselection interview will often be carried out at a local venue or a regional office, prior to the 'head office' stages later on.

One-to-one interviews The preselection interview is quite likely to take this form, and less likely (but nothing's impossible!) to be a panel. Here, there are just two people involved, you (the candidate) and an interviewer. The interview may be highly structured and follow a set script, or very 'open' and appear almost casual in nature. Don't be fooled: a skilled interviewer will most definitely have an agenda to follow even if you appear to be having an informal chat: don't be lulled into a false sense of security and don't be caught off-guard. You may find that the interviewer will take a few notes or fill in a checklist during the course of the interview. Remember too that any interview (not just on a one-to one basis) is a two-way process: if there are things you don't know, don't be afraid to ask.

Panel interviews typically consist of a number of people who will be facing you and asking questions in turn. It is quite likely they will have agreed beforehand what questions each will ask. The panel may be anything from two to six people, each of whom will have some stake in the selection process, and may include a departmental, divisional or section manager, a representative from Personnel or Human Resources, your immediate line manager, or even colleagues from the team. While it may seem quite scary to be facing so many people, from a Human Resources point of view panel interviews are generally considered to be fairer because they draw on a range of opinions and are less likely to be influenced by one individual's bias or prejudices. The panel will be able to cross-check their perceptions of you as a candidate and to compare results. Try not to focus on just one member of the panel such as a chairperson; try to make eye contact with all the panel as they are all listening to you!

Group interviews (inviting a group of candidates along at the same time) are sometimes employed for the final stage of the selection process, although these may also be included in an assessment centre along with other selection techniques (see below). In some occupations (e.g., school teaching) group interviews may be the customary way of filling vacancies, with the successful individual notified at the end of the day. Don't be too indiscreet or casual, though; one of the 'victims' in the waiting room with you may in fact be an observer!

Telephone interviews are now becoming much more common, especially at the early stages of selection. While it is best to regard any telephone contact with a prospective employer as part of the selection process, there are three basic aims of telephone interviews in selection.

1   Shortlisting: here you should expect to be asked general questions about your knowledge of the company, your interests and qualifications. The aim is to assess your level of interest in and suitability for the vacancy, to produce a shortlist which is viable for face to face interviews.
2   Testing: you may be asked personality-test type questions and asked to indicate whether you agree, disagree, strongly disagree, or whatever. This process can be automated with the use of the telephone keypad.
3   Skill assessment: this may take the form of a role play activity where you are asked to sell a product to the interviewer, or to imagine that you are dealing with a dissatisfied customer.

Telephone interviews can last anything from a few minutes to half-an-hour. You should have your CV to hand and perhaps one or two other reference materials, such as information on the company, that you can access without too much paper rustling! Write down some questions you anticipate you might be asked and some bullet-point lists of answers. An employer may telephone you quite unexpectedly, so have the relevant information to hand.

Finally, some more general telephone tips:

1   Practise presenting yourself positively on the telephone. If you can, listen to yourself, on a recording. Have a practice conversation with someone who will be able to give you feedback. You haven't got body language (see below) to help you to present yourself in an enthusiastic manner, but smiling while you talk will (yes, really!) help you to sound interested, as will making gestures while you speak.
2   Try to slow down your rate of delivery. This naturally increases anyway for most individuals when making a presentation or speaking under pressure.
3   Use a land-line not a mobile (cellphone) if you can. If you have to use a mobile ensure that you get good reception and that your battery is charged up, ignore all other calls and texts and focus only on the interview.
4   Try to be upright, even standing, during the interview as this will help you to project yourself more confidently and to breathe more easily.
5   Do not have any distractions during the interview; even a muted television can cause pauses in the conversation that will cause the interviewer to question whether you are giving him or her your full attention.
6   It is much better from your point of view to have the telephone conversation at a pre-arranged time. Make sure that you sound awake and alert during the conversation: if you are drowsy, sluggish, or even hung over this will be very obvious to the person on the other end of the line.

7   If you are calling to confirm that you will attend an interview remember that you may be talking to the person who will actually interview you; don't assume that it will be somebody simply taking a message. If you are told that it isn't convenient for you to speak to them at that time try to identify a specific time when it will be convenient.

8   If you are making an international call remember that while it may be mid-afternoon for you, it may be just before 'close of business' for the person you are calling. Try to work out what time it will be in the other country and make your call appropriately.

Succeeding at interview

Preparation   The six Ps of interviewing are: 'Proper preparation prevents pretty poor performance.' The following list should help you to prepare before you get to the face-to-face discussion:

1   Do your homework. Find out about the employer and the job, and think about how your profile matches the job requirements. You may be able to find information on the organisation on the Internet, in your careers service resource base, or in your university or college library. What are the main issues facing the organisation, the industry or sector at the present time? What trends will apply in the future? What opportunities or threats present themselves?

2   Sort your head out. Try to manage your stress, get an early night the day before the interview, do not drink alchohol the day before the interview as it may make you drowsy and, paradoxically, also prevent you sleeping properly. Get some exercise, practise breathing, and talk about what you are doing with friends.

3   Pay special attention to your personal presentation. In addition to the hints in 'interview image' below, don't drink or smoke before an interview as the smell can still linger on your breath, and smoking is more or less completely unacceptable in work places nowadays. This may be a good time to quit! Be careful what you eat the day before the interview as this too can cause bad breath or stomach upsets.

4   Practise the interview with friends or even arrange a 'dry-run' with a manager in a similar organisation.

5   Plan the logistics: how will you get to the interview, how long will it take, are you 100 per cent sure you can get there on time? How big is the site? You may need extra time to get from the site entrance to the offices. If you are driving, where will you park? Telephone the organisation to enquire. Aim to arrive at least 10 minutes early.

6   If possible, try to visit the organisation discreetly and see what kind of clothes people wear: can you spot differences between managers and the workforce?

7   Take a pen and a small notepad with you as you may think of questions on the way to the interview, or there may be things you need to remember. There is more on interview questions below.

Interview image   Student life is a time when you can have the luxury of being more individual, without the need to fit in with 'business' norms of personal presentation. However, organisations will expect you to fit in with their norms, image and culture. Your potential employer will form an impression of you within the first few seconds of meeting you, and it is generally recognised that most of this 'impression' is based on the way you package yourself. The following points should help you:

1   Wear a suit unless the company has a strong dress-down culture. Don't take risks with what you wear and wear clothes that you are used to and are comfortable in, while still being sharp, smart and new-looking. Don't be tempted to buy a cheap suit. Males should go for a dark, plain business suit (charcoal is good), avoiding loud pinstripes. If you can, buy a new one, as you will probably find that the one you wore for Uncle Bill's wedding two years ago doesn't quite fit any more: too many kebabs or nights in the Union bar maybe? A decent suit needn't cost a fortune, and can be had for under £150. You will get plenty of wear out of it when you get the job! Women should aim to wear something relatively conservative and smart without being prissy.
2   Borrowing clothes is not recommended. You will not feel comfortable, possibly fidgety, and the interviewers will pick this up.
3   Make sure that shoes and fingernails are clean, ties done up properly (a Windsor knot looks great if you can do one!), clothes pressed and accessories co-ordinated. Never wear orange or yellow (too *Austin Powers*, yeah baby!), and avoid pastels for anything other than a shirt.
4   Wearing new shoes for the first time is not a good idea, as they may not be comfortable and you will find the interview process challenging enough without having sore feet. Shoes must be clean and shiny, however.
5   Men should wear dark socks, not patterned and nothing silly!
6   Make-up is essential for female candidates, in moderation. Use light levels of foundation and eye make-up. Use a spot-stick on any offending zits! Men should have a fresh shave (but don't use a brand-new razor) and avoid aftershave as it can sting and may present an over-powering smell. You may use a good perfume in moderation.
7   On the subject of smells, personal hygiene must be absolutely faultless and odour-free, not just breath as referred to above. Avoid sweat patches, even though you may be nervous. If the selection event is especially gruelling, consider having your suit cleaned before you wear it again.

8   Hair should err on the conservative side (nothing too wacky), and again try to find out what the corporate culture would feel comfortable with. While piercing is more acceptable today than, say, in the 1990s, you may wish to consider whether yours will be acceptable in your chosen organisation. Visible tattoos are generally a no-no.

9   Watch your posture! It may be a good idea to video yourself being interviewed as you can get quite a shock. Generally males tend to slouch or be too casual. Aim for a posture that looks confident but not aggressive, try to sit upright and *smile*! You are trying to persuade the interviewer(s) that they should like you, so being pleasant while not overfamiliar should give good impression. There are more notes on body language in the section below.

10   Don't carry too much stuff with you as this can present an image of disorganisation. They are not in the market to recruit a bag-person!

11   Finally, try to avoid the situation where a key interview is the very first time you wear a particular outfit or present your new, well-groomed image. Your clothes and your presentation should be something you feel comfortable with.

Arriving for interview   So, you have arrived, not too early and not too late. Be nice to the reception staff even if they aren't nice to you (I always think of this as a moral victory) as they may be asked for their impression later on. The following tips will help you get started:

1   Visit 'the facilities' on arrival. Not only will you feel more comfortable, it is also an opportunity to tidy up clothes and hair, and to compose yourself before facing any more of the organisation's staff

2   While waiting you may be offered tea or coffee. Handle these with care and don't feel obliged to take more than a few sips. Be aware of crumbs and chocolate on fingers!

3   Think about your posture when you are in the waiting room as well. You are probably still being observed.

4   If there are other candidates it is polite to engage them in conversation (remember they may not be a candidate at all!) but don't try to 'score points' (even if they do), or conversely allow yourself to be hassled by what they say.

5   Never smoke or chew gum.

6   When invited into the interview room, it is polite to knock if the door is closed, and shake hands if you think appropriate. The handshake is a science in itself: for men, not too firm or too limp (yeuch!).

Personal presentation and body language   In the interview itself, posture, personal presentation and body language are very important (with apologies for repetition of earlier information).

1　Remember that the panel probably know nothing about you other than your written application and what they see before them. This is your opportunity to make a good impression.

2　Sit upright, but try to be relaxed and comfortable. Do not fold your arms as this is a 'closed' gesture, indicating defensiveness. Crossed legs can indicate a casual approach, so keep your feet in the ground. It may sound silly, but practise sitting, in front of a mirror, on an upright chair, or better still have yourself videoed in a mock interview, and decide for yourself what looks best.

3　Do not hold a pen or a coffee cup, as this will make you uncomfortable and fidget.

4　Speak clearly and concisely, and avoid 'um', 'er', 'you know', 'yeah', 'OK'.

5　Try to keep eye contact without staring! Look at the person who is asking the question, and try to scan around the other panel members. If you don't feel comfortable doing this, look at their eyebrows: it will look as if you are keeping eye contact even if you aren't.

6　Try to smile (occasionally), be enthusiastic and friendly without appearing too casual or cheesy. Humour is best avoided as it may not go down well.

7　Focus on the questions and, if you don't understand a question, ask for an explanation. Don't interrupt the interviewers. A slight lean towards the questioner generally indicates a focus on the question, as can nodding slightly.

8　'Mirroring' means copying some of the body language of the interviewer. It is a subtle tactic, aimed at encouraging them to believe that you are like them, because interviewers like people with whom they feel they have something in common.

So, what shall we talk about?　You will also need to think about *what* is said. In the previous chapter we emphasised the need to do background research on the organisation, and this is a good time to use the information again. It is a good idea to show, without having to be asked, that you have some knowledge of the organisation and what it does, and have taken an interest in it. Whole books have been written on interview question and answer techniques, but before we think about the detail of those, let us first revisit some general aspects of your skills and personal qualities, to give you the basic information to deal with questions at interview:

1　What are your strengths in relation to this job and this organisation? List the positive points that you believe have got you into the interview, and be prepared to go over these again, if asked, in the interview. Check your CV again and think about how you can talk about yourself, in an organised way, in chronological order if needed, or around certain themes, such as your education, your experience and your extra-curricular achievements.

2　You may be asked what are your weaknesses. There are several aspects to this. First, if there are weaknesses that are clear from your application (e.g., poor results in mathematics) then you may well be asked about these. It is important to state how you are addressing the weakness, without being too defensive. For example:

> Yes. I agree. I was disappointed with that result but I have worked hard at developing those skills since then and feel much more confident with that area now.

3　If you are asked what your weaknesses are, you may wish to think about what are called *allowable weaknesses*. These can be aspects of your personality or skills that may appear to be a weakness but actually show you in a positive light and could also be a strength, or weaknesses that don't actually impact on the job role. For example:

> I think in the past one weakness has been a tendency to get involved in too many things. You will see from my CV that I held positions of responsibility in three different clubs and societies while at school. This was interesting, but it put me under a lot of pressure, and when the examinations came around I stepped down from some of my responsibilities. The experience taught me to prioritise, how to manage my time, and to recognise things that are really important. These are important skills in a managerial role.

Of course, a skilled interviewer may well wish to develop these points and to probe further, so be prepared for a more in-depth discussion of the points you raise!

Interview questions: what will they ask you?　Examples of interview questions, and some suggestions for things that you might cover in your answers, are given towards the end of the chapter. Generally interviewers will use 'open' questions, which are intended to get you to talk openly about yourself, rather than give a yes/no answer. Be prepared to answer questions about:

- your CV or application, and almost any aspect of your history
- what you believe you can contribute to the organisation
- your knowledge of the organisation
- your motivation, career choices and future plans
- your interests and activities
- how you deal with certain situations

Interview questions: what will you ask them?   As this is a 'two way conversation with a purpose', you should expect to ask questions. Here are some basic dos and don'ts:

1   You could ask questions relating to facts about the organisation that you haven't picked up in your prior research. These may relate to its organisation, numbers of employees, or things you have observed on your visit. These might include:
   (a)   how well has the organisation performed in relation to its competitors?
   (b)   what does the organisation believe to be the main challenges facing it in the future?
2   You would ask questions relating to your job. These may include:
   (a)   where will you be working, what will the role involve, to whom will you report?
   (b)   what training will you receive and how does this link to the organisation's training strategy?
3   You could ask questions relating to the management of your placement and any project work you may have to undertake
   (a)   what aspects of the organisation do the panel think you should focus on in your placement project? (This turns the project into a 'consultancy exercise', which organisations like.)
   (b)   will you be appraised during the placement, how often and by whom?
   (c)   when should you expect a decision on your application? What happens after the interview?

However, there are also questions and topics that are best avoided, which include:

   - questions relating to holidays, pay, sick pay
   - discussion of your opinions on issues such as sexism, racism or disability discrimination
   - discussion of political issues, and anything that could lead to a conflict of opinions with the interviewer

You may also need to make an input into the general direction of the interview. If you feel that you are not getting an opportunity to state your case, this may well be due to an inexperienced interviewer who feels that he has to dominate the situation. You will need to gently assert yourself and try to steer the conversation back to a discussion about you in relation to the job.

At the end of the interview, thank the interviewer(s) for seeing you, and end on a positive note, saying, for example, that you look forward to hearing from them. Even if you feel the interview hasn't gone well, you may wish to apply for another position in this organisation at some later date, so leave the interviewer(s) with a positive impression.

After the interview

After the interview is over, and you have some space for reflection, try to think about what went well and what didn't. Most people don't ask for feedback if they are successful, but in fact it would be really helpful to know what worked on that occasion, and ways in which you might improve in the future. Who knows, your next interview may be for an internal vacancy or promotion, so just because you are asking for feedback doesn't mean you are still job hunting!

If you were unsuccessful, you should ask for feedback anyway. Try to see the last interview as a step towards the next one, and as a learning process. You may also have not been chosen for all the wrong reasons, including:

- an unskilled interviewer was unable to spot your obvious talent (steady now!)
- the panel couldn't agree on a selection decision and have decided to re-interview (this one is frustrating, for the organisation too, but it does happen)
- the organisation has decided not to fill the job right away due to budgetary restraints
- the job had already been earmarked for someone else and the interview was just window-dressing (unlikely, but it does happen)

On the other hand, there may simply have been a better candidate than yourself, in which case the best thing to do is to take any feedback on board and try to do better next time.

Assessment Centres

The term 'Assessment Centre' (or 'selection board' in some UK public sector organisations) normally refers to the use of a range of assessment methods with a group of candidates over an extended period, normally up to two days. They are typically but not exclusively used by larger employers, but even small companies may supplement the traditional interview process with, for example, a psychometric test. They are commonly used in graduate recruitment (so you'd better get used to them) and can also be used in selection for sought-after work placements. The characteristics of a typical Assessment Centre are:

- they are often residential, staying in a hotel or training centre, or on the employer's premises
- several candidates can be seen together, in a range of situations, and subjected to a variety of assessment tools
- the activity is normally intensive and demanding, so the employer will have the opportunity to see candidates under pressure, working with other people, and undertaking a range of tasks
- observation is continuous, even during meal times and recreational periods, so candidates should aim to be 'performing' (but not over-acting) at all times

Most candidates report that they enjoy the experience of an Assessment Centre even though they can be exhausting. Some Assessment Centres are part of a much larger selection process, so you may not be in direct competition with the other candidates you meet. This is useful to know; don't be afraid to ask.

The components of a typical Assessment Centre may include the following (in more or less any order).

Information-giving activities

Very often the Assessment Centre will be 'launched' by a presentation or video relating to the organisation, possibly accompanied by written material.

What you should do: try to absorb as much of this as possible and use it as the basis for later questions and discussion.

What you should not do: switch off, glaze over, daydream or not listen.

Team exercises

These normally include a task to be completed, perhaps building a model out of limited resources such as sheets of paper to a predetermined specification. It may also be a paper-based task, such as discussion of a case study scenario.

What you should do: in Adair's 1973 theory of action-centred leadership an effective leader reconciles three things: the need to achieve the task set to the group, holding the team together and building team spirit, and making sure the individual needs within the group are met and that individuals don't feel left out or in conflict with others. Try to:

- take the activity very seriously, even though it may seem silly or pointless (see example below)
- be friendly, and give the impression that you are really involved in the activity
- be creative in your proposed solutions, but not too weird or wacky

- persuade others of the merits of your ideas
- encourage everyone to join in
- resolve conflict within the group
- assert yourself, but in a subtle way
- enjoy yourself!

What you should not do:

- try to impose (force) your ideas on others
- disagree with other candidates just for the sake of it
- criticise or attempt to undermine the other candidates
- tolerate this behaviour towards yourself; it is best dealt with by very politely speaking to the person concerned, in a break, within earshot of one of the facilitators
- agree with other candidates simply because you can't be bothered to work out a solution
- focus to too great an extent on just one other person in the exercise, either in the form of alliances or bullying
- become angry or stressed

Examples of team exercises include:

- building a model vehicle out of paper to a very precise specification: this exercise also assesses the team's ability to meet demanding quality standards.
- building a model out of building bricks that is a copy of another, but which is hidden from most of the team; this also assesses the team's ability to communicate instructions clearly.

Group interaction

Here you will be asked to take part in a discussion or debate. It may be led by a facilitator, or be a 'leaderless' exercise, where you are expected to manage the activity as a group. It is almost always risky to try to guess what attributes the selectors are looking for. Generally many of the points listed above under 'team exercises' also apply here, and especially the following.

What you should do:

- participate enthusiastically
- show that you can be a listener ('positive listening') as well as someone who contributes ideas
- be flexible and be prepared to accept ideas other than your own

What you should not do:

- do not assume that certain attributes are automatically sought for certain positions: that sales positions require you to be brash or dominant, or that human resources positions require you to be either ruthless or 'touchy-feely'
- try to manipulate the discussion

Role play simulations

Here you will be asked to role-play a situation similar to one which you might encounter in the job role, most often used in selection for customer relationship type roles. For example, you may be asked to deal with an angry or aggressive customer.

What you should do:

- deal with the situation calmly and assertively
- try to turn a problem into an opportunity: for example, to make the customer delighted with the help they have received

What you should not do:

- remember that ultimately you should portray the organisation in a positive way, so don't agree too readily with criticisms of the organisation
- allow yourself to be harassed or hassled, or to become angry. If in doubt or if totally out of your depth, then state that you will refer the problem to a senior manager. It may be that you have been pushed too far or that the exercise is not being well managed, or the job may not be the one for you!

Work simulations are similar to role play simulations, and may include, for example, 'in-tray' exercises where you may be given a series of tasks to perform, or to prioritise.

Networking activities

This category includes meeting people from the organisation, taking a tour of the organisation, the mealtimes and coffee breaks during the assessment centre, or a social event. You will be under observation at all times, so it is wise to remember the following points.

What you should do:

- be unfailingly polite, pleasant and cheerful, in as natural a way as possible

- try to take in as much as possible if you are shown round as you will get a feel for the 'climate' of the organisation
- be prepared to ask questions, such as to existing employees about their experiences of working for the organisation

What you should not do:

- overindulge in the hospitality, either food or drink, even if it is free!
- be indiscreet or critical of the organisation in your comments to other people, as the person you are talking to may be an assessor rather than a candidate
- try not to smoke even during breaks, as it is not acceptable in many organisations, and the smell will linger on your clothes and breath
- do not be influenced by someone who expresses very negative opinions; even the most successful organisation can have its embittered employees or whingers
- overall, don't relax too much, and remember that you are always 'on' from the moment you arrive until the moment you leave.

Presentations

You should expect a presentation to be part of a typical assessment centre. It is used to assess your communication skills, the amount of effort you put into a given task, your ability to present information or deal with questions, and it may even be part of the job. As with some other aspects of this chapter there are whole books on presentation skills, but briefly:

What you should do:

- think about who your audience will be, what content you will include, how this will be structured, what visual aids you will use
- think about the beginning (your introduction), the middle (the main part of the content) and the end of your presentation (your summary)
- if you must, have cue cards, but do not read directly from these
- try to anticipate questions and think about how you will answer these
- practise the whole presentation and, if you can, time yourself
- better still, video yourself, but be prepared for a shock!
- make sure you can use any equipment (e.g., projectors)
- think about body language, eye contact, how you move and stand, what you do with your hands
- talk to the whole audience, not just the assessor

What you should not do:

- arrive for the presentation expecting PowerPoint to be set up and ready to use, unless this has been agreed beforehand. There is nothing worse than struggling to coax a slow laptop into life in front of an audience
- don't try to include too much, and don't put too much information on slides and flipcharts; ensure these are legible
- use poorly prepared materials or try to muddle through at the last minute

Because presentations are a commonly used form of assessment in further and higher education, poor presentation skills are more or less inexcusable. If in doubt, work on yours.

Psychometric tests

These are also commonly used in Assessment Centres, as well as a stand-alone assessment and selection tool. While they are often used in the context of an Assessment Centre, this is not exclusively the case, and you may find yourself presented with a test when you attend a job interview. Psychometric tests are (typically) questionnaires, designed to assess your reasoning abilities, or how you respond to different situations, or your attitudes. Your results will be compared with how other people have done, or with predetermined scores which may be linked to carefully specified competences and criteria. The main types of tests are outlined below:

1 Personality questionnaires: these look at your values, preferences, reactions, and attitudes. There are no 'right' or 'wrong' answers.
2 Aptitude or ability tests examine your reasoning ability (your thinking ability) as well as your ability to do specific things related to the job. According to Fagan (2003: 132): 'Aptitude and ability testing are almost identical, the main accepted difference is that aptitude is used to measure a specific ability (perhaps related to a specific job such as IT support) whereas ability is used to measure your general ability.'

What you should do:

- try to do some 'practice' tests beforehand, using the sources listed at the end of this chapter, although your first port of call should be your own university or college careers centre
- try to answer as many questions as possible, but without rushing excessively

- follow the instructions you are given exactly
- read the paper, and especially the instructions, carefully
- if you have time, look over your answers

What you should not do:

- don't try to 'guess' what the selectors are looking for, then try to answer accordingly. You will end up introducing bias into the results and will not present yourself accurately. Unless you are totally honest then the test result will not be a true representation of you, and you could end up being chosen for an inappropriate role!
- don't spend too much time trying to prepare for tests; it is generally better to answer them in a natural way
- don't waste time or get bogged down on difficult questions; if you get stuck, move on
- don't attempt a test if you feel unwell, as you will not present an accurate result; try to arrange another sitting.

Psychometric tests are commonly used but would not be used in isolation. You have plenty of opportunity to practise before the 'real thing', so use it!

As a concluding comment on the subject of Assessment Centres, it is surprising how many candidates approach them with fear and trepidation, yet talk afterwards about how much they enjoyed the experience. However, it is possible to enhance your chances of success by prior preparation, but principally by how you conduct yourself on the day.

ACCEPTING THE JOB AND FOLLOW-UP

Amazing! You weren't sure that the Assessment Centre had gone so well, but here you are reading a letter offering you a work placement. Before you rush to accept, try to work through the following questions, and if the answer is 'yes' in most cases (and the 'no's do not seem too important) then you should accept, albeit with caution:

1 Is it the placement you really want, you really, really want? Or was it one of your 'long shot' applications that has unexpectedly come good?
2 Does the placement meet the requirements of your course or educational institution?
3 Can you afford to do the placement? Does any remuneration meet the living or accommodation costs, which can be a problem in some areas? It is worth taking the time to check this out if you think it may be a problem.

4   What is the typical working week and can you cope with the commuting if required?
5   Does the placement fit with your long-term plans and your overall career aims?
6   What do you expect to learn?
7   Do you feel comfortable with the overall company culture?
8   What does the organisation expect of you and can you deliver this?
9   Have you met your immediate line manager?
10 Will you actually enjoy the placement?

   The offer is likely to be made by telephone, by letter, or during the interview itself. Try to be enthusiastic about the offer even if you still have some concerns. It is normally reasonable to ask for some time to consider the offer. This 'offer' phase is an opportunity for some negotiation if you feel you have the 'room' to do this, but be cautious, and do not expect the employer to agree to all that you request. Let's be realistic: in a placement situation you are likely to gain a lot more than the employer, no matter how well you package yourself, so try to look on the placement as a chance to gain experience rather than simply a job.

SAMPLE INTERVIEW QUESTIONS

In this section we consider a number of possible interview questions, in six categories:

- questions about you as an individual
- general questions
- questions about your application or CV, and your academic history
- questions relating to previous work experience
- questions on your knowledge of the organisation
- questions relating to your future career intentions

In each case we will provide sample questions, with some suggestions for things that you should consider in preparing an answer. We can't provide the answers for you, as each individual is different. Clearly this list is not exhaustive, and a creative interviewer can still present surprises, so be prepared to think on your feet! In each case try to think: 'Is there anything else I can add to this list?' You should also try to brainstorm, with your friends, lists of likely interview questions, then try to think of how you might answer these.

Questions about you as an individual

'Tell me about yourself.'
Think about: your age, where you come from, your family, where you are studying, your hobbies and interests, your positive qualities!

'What do you consider to be your three greatest strengths?'
Think about: the contents of your CV, and what the employer is looking for, then link the two.

'What do you consider to be your three greatest weaknesses?'
Think about: the 'allowable weaknesses', things that could be turned into positive qualities.

'I see that you are captain of the university hockey team. What does this involve?' This question is checking to see if this claim is true, and also inviting you to talk about the valuable skills you have acquired in this position of responsibility
Think about: the team and your achievements, what you actually do as captain in relation to motivation, leadership, organisation, planning, and the task/team/individual challenge.

General questions

'What do you understand by the term "management/marketing/logistics" (or some other business term)?'
Think about: this is your field so you had better have a clear answer! Demonstrating an understanding of what your field of study or the vacancy actually involves shows commitment, and establishes a bond with the interviewer (or at least one of the panel) who may be from that field.

'What do you expect to gain from a work experience placement with this organisation?'
Think about: the opportunity to achieve an ambition, skills, learning, professional development, real world experience, first hand experience of working in this specialism, communicating your interest/excitement/ motivation about the position.

'What should this organisation expect to gain from having you spend a period of work experience with us?'
Think about: your ability to make a contribution to the team, your willingness to learn, your flexibility, your capacity for hard work, particular skills that you have that are valuable to the organisation, possible links back to previous work experience (e.g., dealing with customers).

Questions about your application or CV, and your academic history

'Can you explain why your A-level grades turned out the way they did?' (eg. this may be picking on an area of weakness in your application)
Think about: challenges you may have faced during your A-levels, what you have done since then to improve your academic profile, the high grades you have achieved at college or university.

'What would you most be remembered for at school or college'?
Think about: not just your academic achievements, but especially your extra-curricular achievements. How can you demonstrate that you did more than just attend classes, that you really took part in the life of the institution, that you made a real contribution, 'citizenship'.

'Why did you choose your present course?'
Think about: a positive statement demonstrating a commitment to the field of study, rather than simply something that either seemed a good idea at the time, or you couldn't think of anything else to do! The opportunity to do a work experience placement, the employability record of previous graduates, the content of the course?

'Why did you choose to go to (your) university or college?'
Think about: again, a positive statement about the things the institution offered, its reputation, the impression that you gained of the institution on open days or when you visited, the distinctive content of your course, the strength of the university, course or subject 'brand' in the employment market place, the commitment to work experience. Never: 'It was the only place that accepted me!'
Why did you choose to go to university as opposed to, say, going to work?

'I see that you took a gap year. Please tell us about this.'
Think about: the skills you gained the experience you gained, planning and organisation, overcoming challenges, feeling prepared for career stability.

Questions relating to previous work experience

If you have prior work experience (perhaps you worked full time for a year after leaving school, or perhaps you have had significant part-time experience) then your interviewers may well be very interested in this. It can say a great deal about your ability to cope with the challenges of the work place, and the world of work generally.

'I see that you have worked part time in a retail store/call centre/pub/ nursing home. What do you think you gained from this experience?'
The interviewer is interested in whether you can see jobs, even quite mundane jobs, as learning experiences.
Think about: dealing with customers, colleague relationships, dealing with work procedures and quality standards, meeting targets, how you managed your time, juggling the commitment to work and study.

'I see that you have worked full time for one year. Tell me about that.'
The interviewer is interested in why you did it in the first place, what you learned from the experience, why you quit!
Think about: your original reasons for taking the job. It is OK to admit to a lack of focus in the past providing you can demonstrate that you are focused now! Turn this question into an illustration of your real commitment to the field of study and area of work.

Questions on your knowledge of the organisation

'Why did you choose to apply to this organisation for a work experience placement?'
Think about: the reputation of the organisation, the strength of the employer 'brand', the added value to your CV from being associated with this organisation, the 'fit' with your career intentions, the opportunity to acquire skills and knowledge.

'What do you know about our business/products/markets?'.
Think about: the prior research you did, products and markets, well known brands, recent history, what you know of their future plans, market segmentation, product life cycles; emphasise the strength of their reputation as an employer and as an organisation generally.

'Who do you see as our major competitors?'
Think about: your market knowledge, presenting the organisation positively but realistically in the context of the main competition, challenges for the future.

Questions relating to your future career intentions

'Why did you choose this type of work experience? How does it fit with your career plans?'
Think about: how you can demonstrate your commitment to this area of work, how it fits with a long-term plan (actually, even having a career plan

is quite rare so this will make a good impression!). Placements can sometimes turn into longer-term career opportunities but don't assume this.

'What do you see yourself doing in five/ten years' time?'
Think about: again demonstrating your commitment to the field of work, but also to your continuing professional development or CPD.

COMPETENCY-BASED INTERVIEW QUESTIONS

Well-trained interviewers will ask questions that will help them identify if you are able to do the job, whether you are motivated to make an effective contribution, and your 'fit' with the organisation. Competency-based interview questions relate to how you would behave in certain situations, either from your past experience, or based on what you have learned and how you would now do things differently. Selection processes are often based on an analysis of what has made for successful employees in the past. This 'blueprint' will be presented to you in the form of the job description or person specification, if there is one. You can analyse this to identify what you believe the organisation is looking for.

Many of the questions above could be developed into competency-based questions, as in the example below. Questioning in competency-based interviewing normally has a number of components:

- an 'introduction question': this introduces a new topic or line of enquiry
- a series of 'probing' questions, which aim to clarify what you have said or explore the issue further
- a 'linked' question, related to the main issue but tangential to the main line of enquiry

For example, an introduction question would be something like 'Please describe a situation where you have had to resolve a conflict.'

Probing questions may take the following forms:

- 'How did the conflict arise?'
- 'Why did you have to resolve the conflict?'
- 'How did the individuals concerned respond to our intervention?'
- 'What did you do to try to resolve the conflict?'
- 'What was the outcome?'

A linked question might be 'How would you say you normally respond to conflict situations?'

Here the interviewer wishes to ascertain whether the interviewee can handle conflict situations appropriately, as clearly this is a major part of the job role. It would be in the candidate's favour to be able to:

- demonstrate an understanding of why the conflict arose in the first place
- provide a rationale as to why his role required him to intervene
- show that he had the personal credibility to persuade the individuals who are in the conflict situation of his ability to resolve it
- demonstrate a planned approach to conflict resolution, taking into account the needs of the different parties
- show that the solution was sustainable

It would count against candidates if they:

- dismissed the conflict as unimportant
- attempted to force their views on the other parties
- promoted only a short-term solution,
- attempted to pass the problem on to someone else even tho-ugh it was their responsibility, and within their ability, to deal with it

The linked question would demonstrate how well a candidate coped with a change of direction in the interview, her personal flexibility, and her ability to think on her feet.

Probing is a common technique in recruitment interviewing, so don't worry about it. The interviewer is interested in real-world examples and your ability to reflect on your experiences and apply these to problem situations. Stay focused on the question and keep your answers concise. Try to remember the things that are on your CV, and what you learned from these. Good luck!

Further reading and resources

There are a range of AGCAS leaflets that should be available in your university or college careers service on interviews, psychometric tests, etc., and some careers services will offer the chance to do 'practice' tests, and even mock interviews. Make use of these!

Many of the career-related publications, such as Hobson's and Prospects, have short sections on how to deal with selection processes in their general texts.

Videos

Many of the video resources relating to interviewing are from a Human Resource Management point of view; nonetheless, these can be useful in a 'know the enemy' sort of way. Your library may well have some of these, such as the ever-popular Video Arts series.

Also check out:

'Why ask me that?' (AGCAS video). This looks at the ways you can deal with initial interviews and Assessment Centres.

'Two whole days', AGCAS Video, on Assessment Centres.

'The Assessment Centre', AGCAS.

Books

Adair J. (1973) *Action-Centred Leadership*, London: McGraw Hill.
Bradbury A. (2000) *Successful Presentation Skills*, London: Kogan Page.
Barrett J. and Williams G. (1981) *Test Your Own Aptitude*, London: Kogan Page.
Byron M. and Modha S. (1998) *How to Master Selection Tests*, London: Kogan Page.
Cohen D. (1999) *How to Succeed in Psychometric Tests*, London: Sheldon Press.
Eysenck, H.J. (1988) *Know Your Own IQ*, London: Pelican.
Fagan A. (2002) *The Brilliant Job Hunter's Manual'*, London: Pearson.
Wilson M. (1995) *How to Succeed at Assessment Centres*, London: Trotman & Co.
Yate, M.J. (2001) *Great Answers to Tough Interview Questions*, New York: Kogan page Adam.

Internet resources

The following are some web sources which include examples of questionnaires for you to try:

www.graduatecareersonline.com/advice/employability/psychometrics.asp
www.hobsers.co.ok
www.intelligencetest.com
www.mensa.com
www.personalitytype.com
www.prospects.ac.ok

Part III

Starting work, surviving and getting on

8

Managing your placement

By the end of this chapter you should be able to:

- be prepared to start your placement
- be an effective worker and make the most of the opportunities for learning
- apply further interpersonal skills, assertiveness and negotiation
- record your skills with evidence in the work place using the PINT framework of skills
- avoid some of the potential pitfalls of employment

INTRODUCTION: A WHOLE NEW CHAPTER IN YOUR LIFE

Congratulations! You have now got your placement sorted and are anticipating starting work and earning some real money. The next questions are likely to include the following aspects:

1   What do I need to do before starting work?
2   What can I expect when I get there?
3   How will I survive?
4   What should my employer expect from me?

This chapter will offer some advice and guidelines to help you be a success and make the most of your placement experience.

Note:

If some of the following cautions seem a bit bleak at times, please don't worry. The overwhelming majority of placement students have a really great time at work and often don't really want to come back to studying. However, the prospect of starting your first full-time job in a new environment can seem daunting, especially if the employer is very large and things seem a bit impersonal at first. Occasionally, placements can be problematic in the first few weeks and whilst the advice below might seem to verge on overkill in places, we want you to have the best possible start. The golden rules are these.

1   It is not unnatural or unusual to feel apprehensive when starting a new job.
2   You don't have to put up with a situation that is dangerous or that exploits you.
3   If you are concerned don't sit back and do nothing. Speak to your work supervisor first and then your visiting tutor. Try to resolve things sooner rather than later.

BEFORE YOU START WORK

Check that you have received and replied to your job offer

Be courteous at all times. The application mind-set shouldn't stop now. If you receive any job offers after accepting your first choice then decline politely and promptly. Times have been good for the economy recently but there are already stories starting to emerge of some across-the-board cutbacks in student intakes, sometimes occurring just before people actually start work. You may need to go back to your second choice.

On the other hand, don't let anyone pressure you into accepting the first job offer that comes along. It has to feel right to you. If you are waiting for the outcome of other interviews then by all means stall just a little bit, but do it positively and politely. You can stretch things out for a week or so sometimes but don't tell your prospective employers that you are expecting another (better) offer. You could look pretty silly if you don't get the alternative offer!

If you do accept an offer but then your dream job happens to come along, talk things through with your placement manager. Employers do understand that this happens sometimes. But whatever you do, don't simply fail to turn up to start work. Whilst you are unlikely to get sued you will, nonetheless, cause considerable inconvenience to the work team that were expecting you to join them. It is real people like yourself that you will be letting down. Furthermore, you will cause a good deal of embarrassment to your university and perhaps even harm the prospects of next year's students. Anyway, that's enough of the lecture (we're wearing our tutor hats again).

Comply with any documentation that your placement office needs

This will usually be in the form of a 'clearance to start' form or similar which enables your university to verify:

- your employer's address together with your supervisor's contact details
- your placement address, e-mail contact and telephone details
- your employer's compliance with the provisions of the various Health and Safety at Work Acts (HASAW); see below

---

Health and Safety at Work

This is very important and more detailed information is available on the UK government's website at www.hse.gov.uk.

Under this legislation **all parties** to the employment have obligations to ensure safety in the work place and this can extend to your university.

Please treat this matter seriously since it is not simply another case of bureaucracy gone mad, even if an office job seems low risk to you. HASAW ensures that it is as safe as possible and stays safe. Moreover, many students will be working in a wide variety of environments such as in laboratories, agriculture and factories and in the service sector in hotels, restaurants, etc.

Check correspondence from your new employer

These may include the following:

- job offer
- joining letter

▓ job description or plan for organising the placement
▓ contract of employment

Apart from the first item, the formal job offer, you may not receive any of these. Often they will be given as your employment starts. If you do receive them in advance make sure that the job and conditions that you thought you were agreeing to at the interview are consistent.

Don't find out later that the 'dream' job in marketing and promotion turns out to be working in a call centre 40 hours a week at an office miles away. If that's not what you agreed to then the best time to say no is before you start. Note that this is a nice illustration of taking the opportunity to take notes at the interview!

Not all employers will issue detailed information in advance of your employment actually commencing. Perhaps the exact position/ tasks they have in store for you won't be confirmed until you actually arrive. This shouldn't be seen as a negative thing, though. Some students say that highly structured placements can be restricting when compared against the experiences of other students who have enjoyed highly dynamic and exciting situations. Make sure, however, that there are mechanisms in place to review the progress of the placement.

Get everything possible sorted out before you start work

This includes items such as a National Insurance (NI) number, if you haven't worked before, your P45 (certificate of earnings and tax/NI deductions made by any previous employer in the current tax year). Things could be hectic when you start and it will take you some time to adjust to your new role and setting. There are a couple of ideas below about accommodation and council tax. If you are moving to a new area you'll find most large employers very helpful in this respect, if you ask them. They may even be able to put you in contact with the previous year's students (who may be vacating their accommodation the week that you will be moving in). But don't think it ominous if they can't always be so helpful. Maybe they have not had placement students before or the person in charge is new to the job; it's always worth asking the question, though.

Working overseas

If intending to work overseas then get any visa applications, work permits, passports, inoculations, etc., sorted out well in advance. See Chapter 10.

Moving to a new area

If you are moving to a new area, or even going to work at a location that wasn't at the same location as the interview, then try to visit it before you start work. Ask your new line manger if it's all right to pop in at some stage. Your new employers are hardly likely to spurn your enthusiasm and professional approach. This will help you to sort out your travel plans, especially if you travel at what will be your normal time. Preparation will help remove some of the worry of being late on your first day. Occasionally it may be the case that the local office is very different from the corporate offices, say, in London, where you had your interview. If the reality is too different from your expectations then it may be best to decline politely now. But, as always, talk it through with your placement manager.

A couple of frequently asked questions

'Is there any help available for finding rented accommodation?'
Always ask your employer first: the Human Resources Department may have a list of approved accommodation. Failing that, look in the local newspapers and estate agents. Also try contacting the accommodation office of the nearest college or university. They may have accommodation available at least until late September. Alternatively, they might be prepared to give you some leads to local letting agencies or their list of approved landlords. Of course, their first priority will be to their own students but some universities do have spare capacity from time to time.

It is not generally a good idea to share accommodation with other students who are not also on placement. The demands of student life and working life can be hard to reconcile when you are the only one getting up at 7am! Think carefully if staying in the same area.

'How do I organise exemption from Council Tax during my placement?'
Exemption certificates confirming that you are a full-time student are usually available from your own university once you've paid your academic fees for the coming year.

DURING YOUR EMPLOYMENT

The main issues are:

- settling in quickly and doing a good job for your employer
- monitoring and recording the progress of your placement
- liaising with your placement office

What will my employer expect?

Whilst out on placement you will be expected to conform to standards of behaviour expected by your employer. This should not be a cause for concern but you may find that the world of work is very different from life at university. Generally, such things are common sense and you may receive specific guidance from your employer, particularly where there is a strong corporate culture or formal code of conduct. Sometimes, though, very little formal guidance may be given; a mature, disciplined outlook will simply be expected.

Adjusting to working life make take time but the following guidelines suggested by various employers over the years provide a general outline of what may be expected:

1 Follow the specific terms and conditions of your employment.
2 Be punctual at the start of the working day and throughout.
3 Always arrive back from any breaks on time.
4 Be well groomed and adhere to the company dress policy (usually smart business dress).
5 Seek out the company rules and staff policies and follow them. There may be a staff handbook or web page for these. For example, most organisations have formal procedures (accompanied by need to fill in various forms) for booking leave, certifying absence through sickness, etc.
6 Always be courteous, polite and professional.
7 Display a willingness to take the initiative (but not exceed your authority).
8 Understand and fulfil each task allocated (it helps to keep a jobs list).
9 Share ideas: offer positive feedback to peers.
10 Have a questioning approach to identify opportunities, challenge the status quo and always ask if unsure.
11 Be diligent. Any errors or omissions in your work may have financial implications for your host company.
12 Keep your employer's affairs and data strictly confidential.
13 Remember you are representing your university and the employment prospects of future students.

If you are asked to do anything that you are unsure about or you feel that you don't have the experience to do then, as ever, the golden rule is 'If in doubt, ask!'

What can I expect?

As a placement student you have a right to be treated respectfully and as an equal employee of the organisation that you are working for. You may not qualify for bonuses, membership of the pension scheme, etc., but it is in the interests of employers to take an interest in your well-being and development. Not only do happy workers do a better job but they may want you to return after graduation. In some cases they may even sponsor your final study year at university.

If you have been open and clear at the interview about being a placement student and you have explained what this entails then you can expect them to be understanding of your ability and development needs. However you must appreciate that routine work will usually form part of your job, especially at the outset.

A word about 'macho' management

Unless you are employed in an industry with its own particular demands then you will typically be working between 35 and 40 hours a week, on a 9am to 5pm basis. The tourism and catering sector is one notable exception to this where evening and weekend working are a part of the job. You should still have time for plenty of life outside work, though. Chapter 2 talked about some of the changes that are taking place in organisations and often there is a fine line between excitement and pressure. Such pressure can easily become stress for managers, and in some instances this can impact on placement students.

Increasingly, there seems to be a sort of macho culture (pushed by both male and female managers) where unless you are working as long and visibly hard as the next person above you in the hierarchy, then you must be lazy, uncommitted and unsuitable for the company. In the UK we already work some of the longest weekly hours in Europe and you should not be taken advantage of as a placement student. You are there to experience work and to further your overall learning, not to prove that you can't be broken by some frustrated, middle ranking executive!

Every situation will vary, however. Sometimes flexibility is needed to cope with peak workloads in your department and usually you will get the time back when things are slack. You may choose to be more involved (maybe the experience or the pay makes it worthwhile), but all we are saying is: be aware, be careful and don't put up with anything that seems unreasonable.

BEING AN EFFECTIVE WORKER

How will I know how I'm doing?

Usually, you'll have an appointed supervisor/team leader/manger who will closely supervise your work and progress. In addition, your fellow workers will no doubt be very supportive and will be only tookeen to help you fit in and encourage you.

Most companies have staff appraisal regimes and as a placement student you can expect at least one, and maybe two, formal appraisals. You should not worry about these. If conducted properly they should enable a two-way exchange of information. You get to find out how your manager thinks you are doing and have the opportunity to raise any issues that you are unhappy with (perhaps staff development issues). Appraisals are a good opportunity to get any interim reports and feedback sheets for university signed off.

What if that support doesn't happen?

If a formal appraisal isn't on the agenda then ask for one after 4–6 months. It may be that the company is small or has a very informal culture. If you feel that you need to discuss the course of your placement sooner, then raise this with your supervisor in the first instance and then if necessary with your visiting tutor.

If you feel that you are being neglected by your supervisor and have little real contact with sympathetic co-workers, again raise your concerns with your supervisor. It may not be their fault. Sometimes a central department recruits placements students for the whole organisation and then allocates students to individual supervisors. Sometimes those supervisors haven't been briefed properly and don't fully understand what a placement entails. Maybe they are under severe pressure.

Unfortunately, such situations are not uncommon and you need to take an assertive approach to addressing your concerns rather than worrying about it and ending up being unhappy and frustrated. There may be other situations in the work place when you will need to persuade people to appreciate your viewpoint and for this reason the final section of this chapter contains advice on assertiveness and the art of negotiation.

What do I do if things get no better?

Ask your tutor for an early visit. He will be able to help you resolve most issues with employers, but he will also tell you if you have unrealistic expectations of work! Usually the advice will be to stick with the situation. You will not be alone. There are usually quite a few students each year who are unhappy in the initial phase of their placement but who, nevertheless, go on to have a really great placement (with some additional experience of human behaviour).

However, if things are really bad and there is no early prospect of improvement then you may have to think about leaving. If so, then it is better to be decisive and positive than let the situation drift, but keep everyone informed of what you are doing.

Visits by tutors

Whilst arrangements for supervision and assessment of placement vary between universities you can normally expect at least one work place visit (usually in the first half) and a second check (often via the telephone) in the second half of your placement. The work place visit will typically last between one and two hours and will enable your tutor to meet you and your supervisor to discuss the progress of your placement. Your placement tutor will rely on you to make the detailed arrangements for these visits, such as checking that your boss is free, arranging a meeting room and car parking if necessary, and sending clear directions.

It is in your interests to make the most of the visit as tutors can help you to reflect on and progress your placement. This is perhaps the only time in your university life that you are organising things around the tutor, not the other way around. Make him feel welcome: He may have had a long journey to see you.

Your placement office will no doubt have given guidelines as to the format of the visit process, but in our experience each visit tends to be different from the next. Sometimes things are very formal with both the line supervisor and a representative from the central Human Resource department present. Often the order of proceedings is geared to their availabilities, but we suggest something along the following lines:

1   Welcome your supervisor and spend a few minutes explaining what is going to happen and who she is going to be meeting.
2   Introduce the tutor briefly to your supervisor.
3   Discuss your progress in detail with the tutor and complete any paperwork.
4   Invite your supervisor to join the meeting and offer to withdraw to give your supervisor the opportunity to talk confidentially to your tutor.
5   Rejoin the meeting discuss any issues that have arisen from the prior discussion with your tutor.

In our experience step 4 often doesn't happen in practice but, nevertheless, you should take the initiative in suggesting it. It will give your employer the chance to say how fantastic you really are without embarrassing you!

Try to ask your supervisor how they wish to do things. Sometimes he'll be happy to suggest an itinerary. Maybe you'll get a lunch out into the process! If you have something interesting (such as a factory or showroom) on the site then arrange to show your tutor around.

All we want to reinforce is that you prepare in advance any assessments/documentation required and that you talk to your supervisor (and if necessary your tutor) about any concerns or issues that you might have. Don't 'drop a bombshell' at the meeting.

Recording your progress and assignments

Most universities will recognise the successful completion of a placement year in some way, perhaps by a standalone certificate or diploma or as a weighting within the overall degree classification. Sometimes it's simply a condition of being allowed to proceed to the final year. Whatever the nature of the outcome you can expect to have some formal academic assessment of your learning. Demonstrating what you've learnt can take many forms typically:

1   A diary of tasks and activities.
2   Interim reports of progress reflecting on your intended learning outcomes and actual experience.
3   A final and more substantial report which invites you to explain your employer's business and organisation structure and your role in the organisation, together with a reflection on your learning during the placement and any future development needs that you have identified. You may also be invited to suggest how your experience will feed forwards into your final year of study.

Whatever the specific tasks, the next section will give you some guidance as to how to record your experiences. And as you will not typically be in an academic environment when you do these things, we'll give you some hints as to common issues to address in your work-based reports.

Common issues in work-based reports

1   Include a contents page.
2   Pay attention to spelling and grammar:
    (a) spell checkers are essential and versions of Microsoft Word above 97 will do this automatically, but beware of words such as 'their' and 'there' which are both spelt correctly but incorrect usage will immediately be obvious to a reader;

(b) grammar checkers (e.g., Microsoft Grammatik) should also be employed, but again there is no substitute for careful proof-reading: ask a friend or colleague if you can;

(c) note that there is nothing more worrying than statements such as 'I'm responsible for designing and updating my company's web site', when the whole assignment is littered with misspellings, grammatical errors and poor punctuation;

(d) when two words become one item a hyphen is necessary, e.g., a one-year placement.

3   After a few months your employer will be very familiar to *you*, but spare a thought for the readers of your report:

(a) include some figures and statistics on size, profitability, number of employees, turnover, etc.;

(b) a mission statement or extract therefrom is extremely useful so as to give the reader some scale;

(c) an organisation chart is a must, if only of your department, but identify clearly where you fit in (put headings on organisation charts and diagrams, especially when they are placed in appendices, i.e., away from the text they relate to);

(d) explain any trade or company acronyms the first time you use them (e.g., HASAW for the Health and Safety At Work Act);

(e) pictures of the product or buildings are worth a thousand words;

(f) include the address of the company's web site;

(g) remember that your reports will be invaluable when applying for jobs in the future, by which time you may be forgetting what all the shorthand was about!

4   Include your own e-mail address.

5   We all expect that you will feel very proud of your achievements and the role you are playing at work, but be careful not to sound as though your doing the Managing Director's job. Try to balance your progress with a few examples of things that you had difficulty with, or would do better/differently next time. Life is a learning experience and we are all on a journey of continual progress.

6   Try to provide examples to bring alive your factual statements. For example one student working for a subsidiary of a German company provided the following example of the extent to which the company had a very formal culture, even down to prescriptions on not being selfish with the daily coffee allocation!

'Coffee is dispensed at mid-morning and mid-afternoon on each floor of the office block. Please remember that serving yourself additional cups may mean that others have to go without.'

7 Try to relate management terms to a theoretical definition where appropriate, e.g., 'An informal group is one that develops naturally among people without any direction from the organization within which they operate' (Greenberg and Baron (eds), 1997).

8 Remember to cite the full reference at the end of your text, e.g., Greenberg, J., and Baron, R.A. (1997) *Behavior in Organizations*, 6th edn, Prentice Hall.

9 Don't forget that the PINT framework provides a useful checklist of transferable skills to monitor your experience against.

10 Authority and responsibility are not always the same thing. Authority can be delegated (i.e., passed down the line of command), but responsibility stays with the original executive and cannot be delegated away. This is why company directors can ultimately face imprisonment for actions of the company. However, you as a subordinate can also be made responsible for a task to the peoon who is giving you the authority.

11 'Evident' is a term that causes much confusion; for example within any formal structure an informal organisation will always be eviden'. This could read '... may also be present', but 'evident' means that its existence is *apparent* and can be *evidenced*.

12 Many organisations use a hybrid approach to organisational design, often combining a functional approach (departments so central as Finance, Marketing, etc.) with a divisionalised approach (perhaps organising Operations into five separate divisions by product or geographical regions). Don't assume that it has to be one thing or the other.

13 Don't get carried away with the corporate superlatives, e.g., 'we strive to deal more generically to provide a service to the customer and be more customer focused'. Whilst such phrases are often propounded in mission statements, etc., you should try to explain briefly what they mean (if not immediately obvious to an outsider) and perhaps give an example. Remember Plain English, and say, for example, XYZ is offering a broader range of services but at the same time reorganising the existing divisions into small units dealing with specific customers. It is hoped to maintain customer satisfaction by better understanding each customer's needs' (or whatever).

It is useful to tell a reader why a company is structured/designed in the way that it is. Perhaps the business is very security-conscious due to high value items (e.g., a bank) or valuable information (e.g., contractors to the Ministry of Defence). Such concerns might lead to a necessarily high degree of formality in working arrangements and interpersonal relationships.

14 *DON'T OVERUSE CAPITAL LETTERS OR UNDERLININGS*
This makes things difficult to read. For proof look at modern road signs, which use lower case letters exclusively because they are easier to read at speed.

Checklist for use in completing records of experience

1 How have I progressed (duties, responsibilities)?
2 What do I really contribute to the job and the team? Also think about this one in terms of 'If I didn't do the job or even did it badly, what would be the consequences?' (for the organisation, not necessarily for you personally).
3 Who am I working with? How does the team operate? What changes in organisation or team dynamics have occurred?
4 What ideas have I had for improving things?
5 What achievements have I had (or even disappointments)?
6 What might I have done differently?
7 What have I learnt? What new skills have I acquired? See placement outcomes.
8 What development needs are arising?

This guide is not meant to be exhaustive but may give some food for thought. Remember, the placement is a learning experience. What you get out of it is directly related to what you put in. Record your development for the future. Don't sit in front of an employer in two years' time and say, 'Well, it was just a placement job for a year. It was basically administration more than anything else, but they seemed quite pleased with me!'

EXAMPLE OF COMPLETING THE PINT FRAMEWORK OF PLACEMENT SKILLS

Context

Sheila works in a specialist travel agency employing around 300 people. The company arranges bespoke travel packages to the more exotic parts of the world. It mainly (but not exclusively) deals directly with clients rather than through a network of agents. Sheila is one of eight placement students who were experiencing a number of different aspects of the company's operations during her placement year.

Interim placement report: Sheila's summary

Since last [placement] visit I have worked in the short break and ticketing departments as well as continuing in Asia reservations. Ticketing especially allowed me to see another part of the company.

This department has a lot more pressure in terms of meeting deadlines. Making a mistake in this part of the company can also be a lot more vital as it could affect a client's holiday. Working in short breaks allowed me to learn about a different part of the world. This part of the company works slightly differently to Asia reservations as bookings are usually less complicated they can be completed much easier.

PINT framework for Sheila	Examples of Experience/Accomplishment
Personal Skills	
Self-management	
– Setting personal objectives	Try to answer more calls, make more bookings, increase my revenue and make less mistakes each month.
– Creating a work programme	Plan each day with time for answering calls. Make time for dealing with current clients, completing paperwork, etc.
– Time management	Allocate enough time to activities to allow for proper completion.
– Working to deadlines	Make sure that everything is completed on time especially for late bookings so tickets, etc., can be sent out on time.
– Coping with stress	Not letting awkward/irritated clients and agents affect my performance.
Self-development	
– Creativity	Little opportunity as yet.
– Problem-solving	Try to provide a client with some kind of holiday even if circumstances mean it is not their first choice.
– Ability to reflect on and learn from experience	Learn from mistakes and see them as a learning experience.
– Critical assessment of progress towards objectives	Performance graphs and tables allow me to evaluate my performance. If performance has not been great in a particular month try to seek why and act upon this.

Interpersonal Skills	
Communication	
– Writing reports	Writing reports for university detailing experiences in company.
memos – internal	Internal memos on bookings to let colleagues know what stage the bookings are currently in.
letters – external	External writing to hotels requesting availability and info on room types. Asking ground handlers for info.
note taking	Listening to client details on phone.
– Verbal speaking	Most of my time is spent on the telephone. We all got a two-day course on telephone skills.
listening comprehension	Acting on what clients have requested and ensuring that I have got this right. If I haven't they soon complain when they get their tickets, invoice and tour itinerary.
feedback	Filling in quote sheets as clients give info over the phone and confirming this is correct with them.
– Body language	Communicating to colleagues whilst on the phone.
– Presentations structure and use of visual aids	N/a
audience contact	N/a
handling questions	N/a
Working with and relating to others	
– Negotiation	Negotiating prices with clients. Negotiating solutions with clients on problem baggage weights.
– Personal assertiveness	Putting forward the company's case to problem clients. In some cases refusing to let clients have discounts. Dealing with customers/clients every day over the phone, taking quote request booking holidays,* giving information, solving problems.

Table – *Continued*	
– Dealing with customers/clients	Daily basis – clients will always phone through with queries relating to their holidays.
– Handling queries	
– Working as part of a team	Working as part of a team of 20 in Asia reservations.
– Task management	Every quote or option held becomes a personal task that I have to try and see through to a booking.
Knowledge & Number	
Integration of subject knowledge from studies	Particular areas of sales, marketing, communication, organisational behaviour and IT.
Exposure to other disciplines/ areas of business	Plenty of workfloor experiences that you cannot be taught from a textbook but can only learn through 'being there'.
Use of numerical data	Costing individual itineraries whilst on the phone. My mental arithmetic improved greatly!
Technology – Information and Communication	
– Word-processing	Letters and quotes for clients, faxes to hotels and ground handlers.
– Spreadsheets	N/a
– Presentation Package	Making information for clients look attractive. Leaflets for colleagues.
– Databases	Company contracts are all on databases and are usually consulted for tailor-made quotes on a daily basis.
– E-mail systems	E-mailing colleagues with important info, hotels requesting rooms and info, ground handlers for info.
– E-commerce/The Internet	Receiving and sending out quotes via the company web site.
– Specific applications such as scientific packages, business systems, etc.	Specific packages for the tourism industry; Galileo and ATOP.

N/a = not applicable

*Taking requests for quotations, giving information, solving problems, booking holidays.

Authors' comment on Sheila's report

As you can see the period in the reservations department has been a busy one for Sheila. It appears she has been spending a lot of time on the telephone dealing directly with customers. This is good first-hand experience for this particular industry.

Stints in other aspects of the business did provide alternative tasks and opportunities for learning and development. For example, a feature of the travel industry is that hotels, resorts and transport operators will provide free familiarisation holidays for staff working in agencies and these students would typically get to go free to the area that they are dealing with. On their return they have to do a presentation to the rest of their team so that knowledge is shared, thus allowing them to put their presentation skills into action.

Some aspects of the work seem quite repetitive and there seems to be a feeling that this is quite a pressured environment. The student is acknowledging this and has had to find ways of coping with the pressure.

There is a good range of skills involved in this particular position even though at the outset it may seem quite specialised. Not all the skills have been covered but this should not be seen as a problem, as long as within the overall placement there is opportunity to cover the majority.

There is no such thing as the perfect placement and very, very, few placements will provide opportunities to do everything on a regular basis. What this student may be losing in range during this stint in reservations she seems to be making up for in terms of doing a real job at the sharp end of business, the customer interface, especially if this is within a broader placement structure. That may be important for the career direction she wants to pursue. What she needs to do is to play to the strong and relevant aspects of her experience and be honest about the areas where she has yet to gain working exposure.

TEAM-WORKING: HOW DO I STAND UP FOR MYSELF AND BECOME AN EFFECTIVE TEAM MEMBER?

You will be joining established work place teams and a part of placement experience is to be able to fit in and do the job. This may often entail getting things done with the co-operation of people in other teams and departments. They also have their pressures and priorities and you will find that to get the job done you will have to assert yourself and often negotiate to resolve your needs and their problems. The final section in this chapter looks at what these two skills are and how you can make them work for you.

Assertiveness

Assertiveness isn't simply about being bossy and getting your own way. It is about having a clear idea of who you are and what you want but at the same time appreciating that to achieve your goals you have to respect the rights of other people and accept responsibility for your own actions.

Assertiveness and a sense of individual responsibility will be crucially important in the development of your career. Employers will be looking for evidence of this ability in interviews. If 'assertiveness' seems a somewhat foreign term it is also referred to as maturity, character, personality, etc., although each of these terms can be interpreted in a number of ways.

The following statements will help to explain the concept:

1 **Respecting myself**: that is, *who I am and what I do.*
2 **Taking responsibility for myself**: that is, for how I feel and what I think and do. For example 'I feel angry when you put me down' is *more assertive* than 'You make me feel angry when you put me down.'
3 **Recognising my own needs and wants independently of others**: that is, separate from what is expected of me in particular roles, such as 'wife', 'husband', 'lover', 'daughter', 'son', 'boyfriend', 'girlfriend'.
4 **Making clear 'I' statements** about how I feel and what I think. For example, 'I feel very uncomfortable with this decision.' 'I think it is a good idea to draw up a plan of action.'
5 **Allowing myself to make mistakes**: that is, recognising that sometimes I will make a mistake and that it is OK to make mistakes.
6 **Allowing myself to enjoy my successes**: that is, validating myself and what I have done and sharing it with others.
7 **Changing my mind**, if and when I choose to.
8 **Asking for '*thinking it over*' time**. For example, when people ask me to do something and I need time to consider whether or not to do it, I say 'I would like to think it over and will let you know my answer by the end of the week.'
9 **Asking for what I want**, rather than hoping someone will notice what I want, and then moaning later if I did not get what I wanted.
10 **Setting clear boundaries**. For example, 'I know that you would like me to visit you, and thank you for the invitation. However, I cannot come this week-end, but would like to come to visit you later this year.'
11 **Recognising that I have a responsibility towards others**, rather than being responsible *for* others. As adults we have responsibility towards and for our children. This is not the same as adult-to-adult relationships where we have responsibility *towards each other* and *not for* each other.
12 **Respecting other people** and their right to be assertive.

Negotiation

Negotiation is an important part of business and everyday life. Ever since we first swapped comics for sweets (or whatever) in the playground we have been negotiators. The usual image of a negotiator is often an Arthur Daley or Del Trotter character, living on his wits to buy cheap and sell (a lot) higher, usually at the expense of some poor unsuspecting customer.

The reality, however, is that negotiation should be about a win–win outcome for both parties, perhaps giving something that is inexpensive or easy to do for you in return for something which you value from the other person:

Example

'Can I have a reduction on that hotel room?'

'No, why should you?'

'Well, I'm prepared to pay in advance and I'd like some friends to join me for dinner. They may also want to stay here.'

Paying in advance (if you have the money) may not be a cost to you and neither is the extra revenue that your friends might spend, but both are likely to be valuable to the hotelier.

Here's an example that is more typical of getting on with people at work:

Example

Marketing department (sales) 'Can I have your department's figures by the due date; this Friday?'

'No! We're too busy – it will have to be Monday.'

At this stage there is little room for movement. Both parties have outlined their positions and, if nothing further happens, both will lose out. One won't get the figures; the other may incur the wrath of the Marketing Director ultimately. Whilst one department could 'win' by 'bullying' the other party, a compromise might sound something like:

'*If* you can give us the overall sales totals for each product by Friday lunchtime *then* we will tell you which individual products we need detailed sales transactions for. That should cut down the work for this week, and *if* you could agree to provide the remaining details by Tuesday, we will then hold a meeting between the two departments to resolve any problems.'

(Response from Marketing)

'OK, *if* the Marketing Department will provide us with the sales codings and orders earlier each week and simplify the despatch system which has become unnecessarily complicated, *then* we will agree to produce the figures. We will also need your support in getting approval to replace the two members of staff who have recently left.'

And so the discussion might go on, until a firm agreement is reached. Note the two key terms '*if*' you will do something '*then*' I/we will.... Do not concede anything unless you get something in return. The keys to negotiation, like many things in life, are *preparation, planning* and *experience*.

For further information read the next sections on the three outcomes and five stages of negotiation. Learning to be a successful negotiator takes time and practice but your expertise will rapidly improve if you think about it as a logical series of steps.

The three outcomes of negotiation

Characteristics of win–win situation (situation focus)

Achieved by a joint discussion and a desire to:

- meet the needs of both parties
- reach a decision that is acceptable to all
- achieve two-way communication
- create flexible approaches
- concentrate on objectives
- maintain a long-term relationship

Characteristics of win–lose situation (domination)

These include:

- 'them and us' attitude between the parties
- each party's energy is directed only towards victory
- a personalised conflict is created
- emphasis is on short-term concerns (long-term relationship is forgotten)

Characteristics of lose-lose situation

These include:

- objectives of either party are not achieved
- frustration of both parties
- long-term relationship is harmed
- no solutions generated or progress made

The five stages of negotiation

Preparation	Decide what you want to achieve. Consider any fall-back position. What would you accept as a minimum? How many ways can these be achieved? What scope is there for variation?
Planning	Plan your approach, and your opening gambit (tactic). Maybe raise the less contentious issues first, or ask for something completely unreasonable to make your eventual position sound extremely fair! Assess the objectives of the other party. Assess what divides you and areas of common ground. Anticipate the other party's likely response to each of your issues, and prepare answers. Give a thought to location: your territory, theirs or somewhere neutral, such as the coffee bar?

Discuss and explore

Introduction	Be sociable and set a co-operative and positive tone for the meeting. Confirm both parties' broad objectives and feelings. Listen carefully for any surprises, and how they affect your plan. Confirm your planning.
Background	Review proceedings leading up to the meeting. Iron out any differences in 'facts'.

Propose your solution

Present your case	Specify in detail what you wish to resolve. Do this in a way that doesn't 'box in' the other party, but don't appear weak. Link issues where appropriate to the other party's objectives. There are many strategies and tactics. Start by setting out your position and asking for what you want.

Persuade and bargain

Negotiate	Link any compromises to other objectives: don't give way without achieving something in return. Remember the key words, *if* and *then*.
Sum up	Summarise the agreement as you see it and confirm the other party's understanding, but don't try to introduce new things and terms just because you feel like you are winning. You will lose their trust and risk destroying the progress so far.
Agreement	Agree on what you have agreed. Eventually, both parties will have to deliver what you have both agreed and both parties need to be happy with the agreement.

Close

Reconfirm	Check that both parties understand the agreement and, where possible, write it down.

Further reading

Two further examples of experience records are shown in Appendices 4 and 5.

9

Making the most
of your potential

By the end of this chapter you should be able to:

- understand the concept of 'employability' and its role in sustaining your career
- recognise the components of employability and how you can positively influence these
- understand the importance of proactively managing your career to achieve career success and consider strategies that will help you do this
- recognise the need for continuing professional development and the relationship this has with the sustainability of your career

WHAT IS MY EMPLOYABILITY AND
WHY IS IT IMPORTANT?

The word 'employability' is used in a variety of contexts, with a range of meanings, but here we are using it to refer to your ability to get the job or placement you want, and to keep the job you may have in the longer term. It has also been widely used by governments, academics and human resources practitioners to refer to the 'employability skills' of an organisation's workforce: that is, their ability to withstand changes in the labour market both inside and outside organisations. Here we are looking at employability from the point of view of you as an individual: the common factor in all these meanings is that it relates to the sustainability of an individual's career.

Why should this be important? In Chapter 1 we discussed the need for 'active management of your destiny', and in Chapter 5 we identified changes that would affect your chosen area of work over the next 20 years. As we identified at the time, if you are a young undergraduate that will not even take you to mid-career, by which time there may have been major changes in your industry, in national and international labour markets, in technology, or in your profession.

There are a number of studies into aspects of employability. Lane *et al.* (2000) and Rajan *et al.* (2000) identified different individual approaches to future careers, categorising individuals as:

▨ *career builders*, who aim to build a career within an organisation
▨ *job satisficers*, whose focus in life is principally outside work, which is simply a means to an end
▨ *franchise builders*, who want to make an impact and build a reputation or 'personal brand'
▨ *flexible workers*, loyal only to themselves, who receive or expect little support from employers

These four categories represent quite different emphases in career terms. Career builders seek a traditional, organisationally located career, and may value job security most highly. Franchise builders would aim to develop what is called in the academic literature a 'boundaryless' career: that is, they would see their career as mobile across a range of organisations, and themselves as independent professionals very much in charge of their own destinies. Flexible workers come and go from jobs as they please, perhaps working for an agency or in a consulting role, although they will still need to build a network of relationships. Finally, job satisficers are primarily interested in lifestyle, although it is still possible to achieve this through work. One could be a ski instructor in the winter and a watersports coach in the summer!

Activity

Which of the above categories would you see yourself fitting into in five or ten years' time? Would you be happy with this?

Within the academic and practitioner literature, key themes in relation to employability include:

▨ an emphasis on individuals taking responsibility for their own career, and on personal growth and self-renewal

- a mind-set that is more in line with self-employment than being employed in an organisation
- where individuals do not expect to have a 'job for life', they must recognise the need to stay employable, and to stay in demand
- the need for resilience in the sense of 'career resilience', as a similar concept to stress resilience
- a positive attitude to change

As a graduate, who is likely to become a professional in the future, you should be well placed to secure your own 'employability'. You can do this by working on four basic areas (see Figure 9.1):

1   Yourself as an individual, specifically your knowledge and skills, your ability to deal with selection processes, how aware you are of job opportunities, how good you are at networking, and how well you perform in your job.
2   Opportunities inside the organisation you are working in, keeping up to date with these, networking internally, how well your occupational group is regarded in your organisation, and your reputation in the organisation.
3   Factors relating to your chosen occupation and career: the demand for your area of work is less under your control, but your ability to keep up to date with the changing nature of knowledge in your profession is (see the section on 'Continuing professional development' below).
4   Factors relating to the external labour market: your awareness of opportunities outside the organisation, your networks outside the organisation including professional networks, and your ability to deal with selection processes in other organisations.

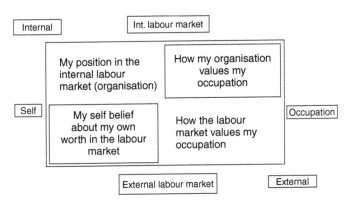

Figure 9.1 The employability matrix: internal and external employability (reproduced with permission) (© Rothwell 2004)

How can you assess your own employability? The questionnaire below is intended to help you diagnose your strengths and weaknesses in this area. Complete it, score it, then reflect on your responses to each individual item: this will tell you much more than the overall percentage score. You can enhance your employability by working especially on those areas where you have gained a low score, and continuing to develop all four 'dimensions' of your employability: yourself, your position in your organisation, your professional profile, and your awareness of the external labour market.

Employability questionnaire for students who are undertaking full-time study

Sixteen statements make up this questionnaire. For each of the statements you should score 1, 2, 3, 4 or 5, where:

5 = strongly agree
4 = agree
3 = neither agree nor disagree
2 = disagree
1 = strongly disagree

When you have completed the questionnaire you will find further instructions at the end of it on scoring and feedback.

Statements

1   I could go for more or less any job in any organisation and get it so long as it was reasonably relevant to my qualifications and experience.
2   There are only certain occupations that are relevant to my skills and qualifications.
3   The success I have in applying for jobs is more due to my personal qualities than my choice of degree course.
4   I am confident that I have made the right choice of course and career.
5   I chose my course without really thinking about future career decisions.
6   I chose my career even though it is apparently unrelated to my course.
7   I think I have been realistic in my aspirations.
8   It is important to be aware of what the demand for graduates is generally when looking for work.
9   I could apply for almost any graduate job and get it, even if it was not related to my degree.

10 If I was reasonably selective about the jobs I applied for I am confident I could get the job I want easily.

11 It does not matter about the qualifications you have or the job you choose; if you are highly employable then you will be successful in finding a good job.

12 How successful you are in finding a good job depends more on the state of the external labour market than your choice of degree or occupation.

13 It is important to get the right mix of qualifications and occupational choice if you are going to be successful.

14 You must choose the right career if you are going to get the job you want; this is much more important than your personal qualities or qualifications.

15 If the recruitment market for graduates is in recession, then I have little chance of getting a job.

16 The career I have chosen means I will be in great demand in the external labour market.

When you have placed a rating of 1, 2, 3, 4, or 5 next to each statement, briefly write down why you have given the statement this rating.

Overall, what conclusions would you draw from your questionnaire results about:

- your perceptions of your future employability
- what you have to do to try to enhance this
- what you can start doing *now*: possibilities include:

  – your work placement (work experience placements are excellent employability-enhancing strategies)
  – developing personal networks in organisations or occupations of your choice
  – identifying the professional organisation in your chosen occupation, and possibly joining it as a student member

CAREER SUCCESS: WHAT IT IS AND HOW TO ACHIEVE IT

Intuitively, one might expect that a topic such as 'how to achieve career success in your chosen field' might be a compulsory part of most vocational degree or diploma courses. It is not. There is a body of academic study on the subject, going back over 20 years, and a visit to a high street bookshop will reveal that there are a number of glossy publications that promise to equip you with career-enhancing strategies. What hardly exists at present is a tradition of an academic study of career success factors aimed at you, the student. The following section aims to rectify this omission, and we hope that it will help you focus on your own long-term plans and intentions.

What is career success?

Surely everyone knows what career success is! Actually, it means different things to different people. Academic studies suggest that there are two types of career success: objective, and subjective.

Objective success is visible, observable, and easily measurable. It is the important-sounding job title (Managing Director, Chief Executive Officer), the six-figure salary, the position at the top of the organisational hierarchy, the size of one's budgetary responsibility, the status of your car in the company car park, and the 'territory' that you control within your organisation. Objective success is there for all to see: it is an external measure.

Subjective success is measured by the individual, within themselves. What we see as 'success' means different things to different people. An individual may have the six-figure salary and the expensive car, but not regard herself as successful because, perhaps, she believes that she has not yet fulfilled her potential. Another individual may have achieved more modest rewards but be happy with these: his satisfactions may lie outside work, or he may not be materialistic. Subjective success is therefore what individuals believe about any of the items under the 'objective' heading. It can also relate to the following:

1   How well individuals are doing in relation to their 'subjective time-table' (their personal perception of where they expected to be by this stage of their lives).
2   Their perceptions of how well they are doing in relation to the work–life balance they desire.
3   Studies have revealed that one's general life satisfaction including one's relationships are also important here, including relationships with partners, family, friends and colleagues.
4   Finally, the recognition and respect that you receive from your boss, your colleagues, or society as a whole will also affect your perceptions of subjective success.

Clearly we don't yet know how successful you are going to be: that lies in the future. Our individual priorities change over the course of our lives as we are presented with different situations, or different life-stages. We may place a high value on leisure time early in our lives, but place more emphasis on material rewards as we find we acquire family responsibilities. What we can measure at this stage is your attitude (albeit at the present time) to career success, and the priority you place on subjective and objective success respectively, and the questionnaire below should help you do this. You will see that some of the items relate to subjective success, others to objective success, and some to both. What is important at this stage is to identify those things you think are important, and to work on these.

The career success potential questionnaire

The following questionnaire is intended to uncover some of the values and attributes that could potentially contribute towards your career success. It is intended to be used as a diagnostic tool, so that you can pinpoint areas that have the potential for further development. For each of the following statements, indicate your level of agreement with the statement by scoring as follows on a *four* point scale:

4 = strongly agree
3 = agree
2 = disagree
1 = strongly disagree

When you get to the end of the list of statements, you will be given further instructions on scoring.

1   The title of the job that I hold should be a reflection of my status and success.
2   It is important that I hold a position of responsibility in an organisation.
3   I need to have a job with high earning potential and visible rewards.
4   It is important to me to see a continuous growth in my real income and rewards.
5   My career progression should match my expectations of my own achievements.
6   A high calibre individual is never out of work.
7   I will always be highly promotable because of my skills and personal qualities.

8 It is important to keep on target with one's personal career goals, and better still to exceed these.

9 One should try to keep a balance between work and non-work activities.

10 I am learning new things all the time and these contribute towards my feelings of success and fulfilment.

11 I need to be happy with the job I have and the rewards I get.

12 It is important to get the recognition I deserve when I have done a good job.

13 My qualifications profile is one of my greatest assets.

14 I rarely feel that I am intellectually out of my depth.

15 It is important that the organisation I work for helps me to develop my career.

16 My social background has not been an impediment to my career development.

17 I am unlikely to encounter discrimination at work that will be detrimental to my career.

18 I believe it is important to take time out to promote and manage my own career.

19 My goals and values are very clear to me and my career intentions are closely linked to these.

20 I am confident that my personal and professional networks will help me in my career.

21 I try to ensure that I promote a positive image of myself to others.

22 I have individuals on whom I can draw for support and advice.

23 I am not concerned about my knowledge and skills getting out of date because always work hard to ensure this doesn't happen.

24 My work is totally central to my life.

25 My self-perception of success is based on my work-related achievements.

Now add up your total score.

76–100 You value objective *and* subjective success very highly and you are strongly motivated to achieve positive results in your career. Go for it!

51–75 You are moderately well motivated to achieve career success but may need to find a focus for your ambitions. Don't be held back by a lack of clear goals; you have lots of potential, now go and fulfil it!

| 26–50 | You need to put a lot more effort into your career promotion and development. At the moment you are probably expecting things to 'just happen' for you, and you need to be a lot more proactive. |
| under 25 | OK, so you are feeling pretty chilled out at the moment. On the other hand, you may be chronically apathetic. It is entirely possible to be successful without being materialistic, but at the moment you are likely not to use your talents and skills effectively, which would be a pity. You know what these are! |

1   Which do you value most highly: subjective or objective success?
2   How can you achieve this: what is your overall career plan for the next five or ten years?
3   Look at your scores for each individual item. Now compare these with the career-enhancing strategies listed below. Which of these do you need to focus on to get what you want?

What affects career success?

Research in this field indicates that there are two main influences that affect career success:

- our 'career success variables' (attributes relating to our skills and qualities that we can use to our advantage)
- our 'career success investments' (what we can do to enhance, boost or develop these in the future)

What are our 'career success variables'? They are a range of factors, mostly but not all under our control, some of which act positively, and some negatively:

1   Education: what level have we attained, where were we educated, what grades did we attain? Graduates are still, even in the position of oversupply, likely to achieve greater career success and earn more than non-graduates. However, because of the oversupply of graduates a good class of degree is now essential. Where you were educated is

also significant, depending on how highly rated your school, college or university is.

2   Experience: your track record as evidenced by your CV, the extent to which this includes strong employer brands, and evidence of personal and professional growth.

3   Personal and professional networking.

4   Other CV-enhancing strategies such as personal achievement: the Duke of Edinburgh Award is one example that may be an asset early in your career.

5   Intelligence: our IQ score, as measured by standard intelligence tests.

6   Personality: what attributes do we have and how do these fit the attributes seen as desirable in our field or organisation?

7   Our organisation's Human Resource policies: to what extent does it promote from within, and do staff get developmental assignments that will enhance their careers?

The following are negative factors, which may affect us. We may not like them, but in the real world they do exist, and we have to fight against them:

1   Economic and social factors can also have an impact, including the ability of rich parents to secure a private education for their children, or social disadvantage for those from poorer backgrounds. More likely to affect almost everyone are the financial penalties associated with university life in the form of student loans.

2   Discrimination, in a variety of forms, does regrettably exist and does negatively impact on career progression.

3   Similarly, bullying and victimisation at work can have a damaging effect on an individual's career progression, or even their psychological well-being.

Revisit your CV. Using the above as a checklist, what are your career success variables, and how 'healthy' are they? Which do you need to work on? Are there any negative factors that you will have to try to minimise?

How can we influence our career success?

There are a number of career-enhancing strategies we can engage with. As you may gather from the career success variables listed above, to some extent success breeds success; so, for example, the more experience you acquire with top-brand employers, the easier you will find it to access other high-profile opportunities. Working on the 'variables' won't guarantee success, because that depends on how we define it for ourselves (and how hard you work at it!), but the following suggestions should help. You may think of others that are unique to yourself! There are two basic things you can do:

1   Work on your career success variables (any impact you can make on these will enhance your chances of success), and work on your CV, minimising the negatives.
2   Career planning and exploration: very few people ever introspect about their careers, or engage in 'career navigation'. This means planning ahead and strategically steering your career to achieve what you want.

These things sound fine, but what do we actually need to do in practice? The following are some more detailed suggestions that you can start to work on now, and during your work placement:

1   Have clear but flexible goals. Try to develop a five-year plan for your career, and keep this rolling forward (otherwise you'll be totally aimless in five years' time!). Set yourself short-term and long-term goals. You can express this as a chart, so that you will be able to see whether you are keeping up with your 'subjective timetable'. You will need to be flexible, though, as careers are no longer as safe and predictable as they used to be, and you may need to accommodate setbacks or changes of direction. Try to treat these as opportunities.
2   Network. If you know what you want to do and the kind of organisations you want to work in, start to make contacts within these. Your placement is an excellent opportunity to do this. If you believe self-employment may be the way for you to go, make contact with individuals who have done this already, in your chosen field.
3   Impression management. What impression do you give to the people you come into contact with? Would they describe you as positive, well motivated, enthusiastic, someone who is good to be with, someone who can always be relied on, someone who makes a valuable contribution? Your placement is again an excellent opportunity to develop this, not just in your 'host' organisation but with other people you meet. You can also start to work on your tutors and lecturers: you may want references from them later, or for them to act as project supervisors.
4   Be mentored. In a career context 'mentoring' is normally a relationship between a more experienced individual and a less experienced individual, where the former helps the latter to navigate her way in

the world of work, provides advice and guidance, and possibly even supports her career development. This may well be a 'relationship embedded in the participant's day-to-day work' (Arnold, 1997: 86). John Arnold's excellent book has a very good section on mentoring.

5   Skills development and CPD. The enhancement of your personal and transferable skills is one of the main benefits of your work experience placement. Try to undertake a before-and-after 'skills audit'. What do you need to work on and, after the placement, what have you gained? CPD is longer-term professional updating (and is discussed below).

6   Your investment in work. How important is your work in the context of your life as a whole? The most *objectively* (and many subjectively) successful people have work as a central factor in their lives, and they tend to place it before other things in their list of priorities. While we would emphasise the importance of a work–life balance, and condemn the long-hours culture that exists in many organisations, if you wish to be successful you should not underestimate the commitment that this will require. It is up to you to decide the extent to which you wish to buy into this, and the place that work will take in your life overall.

Activity

1   Compile case histories of people who you believe to be successful, either in your chosen field or in any walk of life, including sport. What did they do (actions), or what attributes did they have (assets) that helped them to be successful?

2   Identify strategies that you can employ to advance your own career, towards your own definition of success.

3   Do you believe that there are strategies missing from the list provided?

CONTINUING PROFESSIONAL DEVELOPMENT: WHAT IT IS AND HOW TO DO IT

Many graduates will expect to develop their careers in a professional role. This means:

- developing a career within a specialist area, even a broad one such as Human Resources, engineering, or IT
- perhaps membership of a professional institute and the acquisition of further professional qualifications

- identifying oneself as a professional, with some association to professional status, so that other people might trust and respect you as a professional
- an expectation of some level of professional independence and autonomy: because you have this specialist knowledge, you don't have to be told what to do all the time
- and an expectation of professional rewards: salary, flexibility, and a perception of one's career as being unconstrained by organisational boundaries: being in charge of your own destiny

Sounds appealing, doesn't it? The good news is that it is all achievable; you just have to work at it. The bad (or rather, not so good) news is that it isn't an easy ride; it is less predictable than it used to be, and it is getting harder to sustain. Why should this be?

One of the consequences of the rapidly changing world of work is that the professional knowledge people in work hold about what they do goes out of date more quickly. This may be due to a number of reasons, including:

- technological change
- changes in the business environment including legislation, market changes, prosperity or recession
- changes in the nature of work and careers
- at an individual level, keeping your knowledge and skills 'fresh' so that you are always in demand

Keeping up to date, or better still, ahead of the game, is known as Continuing Professional Development, or CPD. The following quotation illustrates the importance of CPD very well.

> The more a profession is affected by changing conditions, the more continuous learning is needed to avoid displacement and the more frequently different employment opportunities arise. (London, 1996)

Let's think about what that means for a moment. First, the price of failing to 'do CPD' is high: if you don't keep up to date you won't be able to sustain your career. However, the reward for 'doing CPD' is also high, as learning new things will open up new opportunities for you.

CPD is a very important issue right now for professional institutes, as they are concerned about two things in particular.

1   Their own and their members' credibility: the public, clients and colleagues need to be confident that the professional person they are dealing with is up to date, and can be trusted.

2　Encouraging their members to keep up to date, to preserve and enhance the body of knowledge within the profession. Some professions (e.g., medicine and the law) have compulsory CPD: if members don't do it they can't keep their professional membership or their 'licence to practise'. Many other professional organisations, including many of the 'business' professions, are moving in that direction.

What do people do for their CPD? At the time of writing, there haven't actually been that many studies of this. Many 'business' professionals prefer informal, work-based methods to formal 'courses' or further qualifications. Professional institutes generally provide plenty of guidance on this and may even provide a 'learning log' or require the compilation of a portfolio. For the individual the challenge is finding something that is genuinely useful but not too much of a burden. Check out what is recommended in your chosen field.

At the end of the chapter is a questionnaire that will help you evaluate your own attitude to CPD, to think about potential barriers to learning that you might face, and what CPD you will actually engage with.

This is a very exciting time in your lives, and a period in which you face considerable challenges, yet at the same time are presented with some terrific opportunities. A work placement is generally recognised as the best CV-enhancing strategy that you can engage. This chapter has been a look into the future; perhaps even the far future as regards your developing career, but it is included in this book because you can set the foundations in place for your employability, career success and continuing professional development now. We hope that we have emphasised that the three are linked:

1　Employability is about getting the job you want and keeping the job you have.
2　Career success is about identifying your goals, and navigating your career towards these.
3　Continuing Professional Development is about keeping ahead of the game, learning new things, and opening up new opportunities.

Your work placement is a foundation for all three of these, being a brilliant opportunity to get a foot in the door, to network, to explore the kind of work that you might be interested in. While none of us knows what the future holds, if you are in control of your career and in charge of your own destiny, then you are much more likely to enjoy the satisfactions and rewards that you aim for, and to achieve your ambitions. We hope that you have found this book useful, and wish you every success (both objective and subjective!) for the future.

The CPD Questionnaire

This questionnaire is designed to help you assess your own level of commitment to Continuous Professional Development (CPD) and your ability to engage in it. It does not assess your learning style (there is a range of other instruments that will help you do that). This questionnaire is principally aimed at people who are in employment; if you are not in employment just now try to answer it as if you were fully employed, or try it again when you are on your placement, or when you have a job.

Score the statements you see below thus:

high score = 4 = strongly agree
moderate score = 3 = agree
low score = 2 = disagree
very low score = 1 = strongly disagree

Give each of the following statements a score of 1, 2, 3 or 4. Further instructions appear at the end of the list.

1　I need to keep learning new things to keep up to date in my field.
2　My employer encourages me to take part in CPD.
3　If I didn't keep up with new developments in my professional work, my knowledge and skills would quickly get out of date.
4　Most of my learning is from immediate colleagues in the work place.
5　My employer is willing to pay for me to attend external courses (short courses related to my job).
6　My employer has paid for me to take part in professional training.
7　Most of my learning is from documentation about work processes.
8　I am studying towards a qualification so that I can get a better job outside this organisation.
9　I can always have an open discussion about my development at my place of work.
10　My employer takes an active interest in my professional development.
11　My professional development is linked to training needs identified during the appraisal (or 'development review') process.
12　I can spend time during the working day on development activity.

13 Every day I am at work I am learning.

14 I am undertaking CPD to enhance my professional status.

15 I think that the development I receive will give me more employment security.

16 I am working towards changing my career direction.

17 I am working towards staying in this organisation but doing something different.

18 All of my professionally-related development activity does not have to take place out of work time.

19 The personal and professional development I am undertaking is an investment in my long-term career.

20 I am actively engaged in working to enhance my employability.

21 My work place has a culture of learning.

22 I have a mentor who gives me advice and guidance on my career intentions.

23 My domestic circumstances do not get in the way of my personal development.

24 My personal organisation is so good that I have no problem making room in my schedule for learning and development.

25 I know what my intentions are in respect of my professional learning over the next two years.

Scoring the CPD questionnaire

76–100   Great score! Not only are you highly focused on your learning, but you also have a supportive employer and there is little that gets in the way of your learning effectively. Keep this up and you should have little difficulty staying ahead of the game!

51–75   You probably mean well but there are likely to be circumstantial factors that inhibit your ability to engage with learning and development. Try to make sure that you get the support you should from your employer, and try to manage your time effectively to fit learning and development in; it will pay off in the end!

26–50   Don't be complacent! If you are going to keep yourself employable you need to keep yourself up to date. Ensure that you get the support you deserve from your employers as well; they are damaging their own interests by not facilitating your development!

under 25   Wake up! It's the twenty-first century!

Look at the score for each individual item and try to reflect on what this means for your CPD.

1   What do you believe are you main barriers to learning? How can you minimise the effect of these?
2   What are the requirements for CPD in your area of work or profession? How can you do this to meet the profession's requirements *and* your own development needs (and maybe those identified by your employer as well)?
3   Can you identify how your CPD fits into your strategic career plan and will contribute to your employability and career success?

References

Arnold, J. (1997) *'Managing Careers into the 21st Century'*, London: Paul Chapman.

Lane, D., Puri, A., Cleverly, P., Wylie, R. and Rajan, A. (2000) 'Employability: bridging the gap between rhetoric and reality: Second Report: the employee's perspective', London: Create Consultancy/Professional Development Foundation.

London, Manuel (1996) 'Redeployment and continuous learning in the 21st century: hard lessons and positive examples from the downsizing era', *Academy of Management Executive*, 10 (4), 67–79.

Rajan, A., Van Eupen, P., Chapple, K. and Lane, D. (2000) 'Employability, bridging the gap between rhetoric and reality: First Report, the employer's perspective', London: Create Consultancy/Professional Development Foundation.

Rothwell, A. (2004), 'Professionals, CPD and employability', unpublished PhD thesis, Loughborough University.

On the Internet, www.PARN.org.uk is the web site of the Professional Associations Research Network, which promotes good practice in continuing professional development.

10

Further help and resources

INTRODUCTION

This chapter contains a range of further information on some of the topics that we have already covered, together with web links and miscellaneous sources of information to help you in your placement. The supporting web site has additional information together with the updated links should any of the site addresses in this book be changed by the owners. The following topics are covered:

- transferable skills
- placement organisations
- volunteering
- overseas
- job hunting
- self-employment
- miscellaneous web resources
- useful books with short reviews
- health and Safety at Work Act

TRANSFERABLE SKILLS

The Plain English campaign exists to promote the use of crystal-clear language against jargon, gobbledegook and other confusing language. It has an extremely good web site at www.plainenglish.co.uk and is recommended reading before writing CVs, application letters and progress report. Avoid the use of meaningless 'management speak' and general gobbledegook.

Personal and interpersonal skills

Mostly these sites are directed to business contexts rather than education but the principles are usually applicable to everyone.

www.time-management-guide.com is a free personal time management and goal setting guide which takes you, step by step, through various aspects of the time management development process.

http://www.tsuccess.dircon.co.uk/timemanagementtips.htm is a shop window for a training consultancy but has useful information and tips on a number of aspects of personal skills. *Common time wasters* is recommended.

http://www.ianr.unl.edu/pubs/homemgt/nf172.htm has thirteen timely tips for more effective personal time management.

http://www.essex.ac.uk/personnel/Pol&Proc/Policies/stress.html gives a good example of an organisational approach to managing stress, from a caring employer!

http://www.jobweb.org/catapult/Assess.htm is a very useful site that gives advice on career planning and also a number of self-assessment sections.

PLACEMENT PROMOTION ORGANISATIONS AND AGENCIES

See www.fledglings.net. Fledglings promote companies who are currently offering industrial placements and graduate schemes to UK universities and their students. Once registered with the site you will be able to access a jobs board and put your CV on-line for interested employers.

You could also try www.studentemploymentservices.co.uk. This new service has recently been established by Student Employment Services Ltd (SES) specifically to assist employers in employing young people on placement. Have a look at their web site, and remember it may be worth mentioning the service to any employers that say they would love to take you on but have restrictions on their 'headcount' totals. SES will employ in a similar manner to an employment agency, recharging the employer with the cost each month.

On a similar theme, but with a slightly different emphasis, Student Support Services, based in Poole, Dorset, exists to facilitate the employment of students for voluntary organisations. They may be able to make a financial contribution to an employer with charitable status in certain circumstances. They are able to do this as a result of employing a number of students. Donations received from some organisations provide sufficient funds to subsidise other students working in voluntary sectors. If you think that this may be helpful in your situation then suggest that your potential employer or placement officer contacts them on the following.

Gradunet (www.gradunet.co.uk) specialises in bring graduates and employers together. Although aimed at graduates rather than placement seekers, you may find it useful in locating suitable companies in your field.

VOLUNTEERING

See www.studentvol.org.uk. For a good publication on how to make the most from doing voluntary work look at 'The Art of Crazy Paving' published by Student Volunteering UK. The metaphor of crazy paving conveys the idea that in changing times your career needs to be laid by yourself one step at a time in a flexible manner as a pathway to success. The direction may meander and the components of the pathway – the skills, knowledge and experience that you build up on the way – may be irregular but, nevertheless, you will get to where you want to be and have the flexibility to change en route if you wish. The guide on the web site takes you through a 7-stage process of analysis and planning:

The organisation's challenge on its site is: *'want to change someone's life? Then why not start with your own?'* The following extract is reproduced from their web site and gives a good introduction to why you might consider voluntary work either in preparation for, or during your placement:

Student volunteering is a unique opportunity for students:
– to increase their knowledge, skills and abilities,
– to understand and appreciate the diversity of our society, and
– to work in partnership with communities for mutual benefit.

The people and projects that student volunteering groups are involved with vary enormously. The most popular work is with children and young people, but there are many other projects that involve ex-offenders, the homeless, people with disabilities, older people, fundraising, health care, animals and the environment.

Students volunteer for a huge number of reasons from wanting to 'make a difference' to simply having fun. However, volunteers also gain an extensive portfolio of skills and experience that can be crucial after graduation. Developing and recognising skills such as communication, management, problem-solving, leadership and teamwork through volunteering not only develops key skills but also enhances employability.

For a full listing of all the member organisations of the National Council of Voluntary Organisations with links to their web sites go to www.ncvo-vol.org.uk.

WORKING OVERSEAS

In Chapter 2 we suggested that working overseas was not only a great opportunity to experience real life in another country but also something that might give you an edge over less adventurous students when it came to the final stages of the graduate selection process.

In our experience many students are attracted to the idea of working overseas but get bogged down by the difficulty of finding a job for themselves, or alternatively get bogged down in the huge range of possibilities that there seems to be when you start looking. Our advice is to try to narrow your search down to one country and maybe just one type of work at the outset. You can always expand your horizons later if necessary.

Many universities have experience of managing exchange programmes but this is perhaps a question to put at open days. It doesn't help to find out that they can't help in your second year. The following links are suggested as good starting point.

Listed elsewhere in this book, http://www.prospects.CSU.ac.uk (click 'Explore Working Abroad') has comprehensive information about possible overseas organisations that recruit annually.

US–UK Fulbright Commission

This is divided into two parts: *the US Educational Advisory Service* (EAS) (tel: 020 7404 6994) provides objective, accurate information and advice to any student or professional considering study or research in the USA: see www.fulbright.co.uk/eas/index.html. *The US–UK Fulbright Scholarship Programme* (tel: 020 7404 6880) is also responsible for promoting those Fulbright awards that are available to UK citizens to pursue study in the USA, organising their selection processes and administration: see http://www.fulbright.co.uk/about/index.html.

Miscellaneous overseas sites

Council on International Exchanges   http://www.councilexchanges.org/18plus/main.html

Interexchange   http://www.interexchange.org

Campcounselors   http://www.campcounselors.com

Campamerica   http://www.campamerica.co.uk

The latest Foreign Office travel information can be found on-line at www.fco.gov.uk: go to 'services' and then travel or telephone 020 7008 0232/0233.

What about an International Student card?

Students on placement abroad will find an International Student card very useful. You may collect information leaflets and buy your card from the Student Union. However, they have a finite life and you should choose when to purchase it with some care in order to gain maximum value. You may purchase your card whist abroad. Simply log on to www.ISIC.card.com for information about sales outlets. Please note that you will have to produce proof of your current student status (your current ID card or yellow enrolment form):

Leonardo projects

Leonardo da Vinci is the European Community's vocational training programme. It encourages collaboration between organisations involved in vocational training, aiming to improve the quality of training provision, develop the skills and mobility of the workforce, stimulate innovation and enhance the competitiveness of European industry. Individual students cannot apply directly but some universities have funded projects to facilitate placement programmes across national boundaries within Europe under the 'Mobility' initiative.

Beware: accepting a placement overseas is obviously more risky than taking one in your home country, especially if you will not be visiting the site/country concerned before you start work.

The best advice is to make sure that you are completely happy with the arrangements before you leave. The following checklist is not exhaustive but is a minimum:

1   What are the travel arrangements? Who is actually paying?
2   If you decide to return will you have to pay or can you transfer your ticket?
3   Have you been given a clear idea of the standard of accommodation (i.e., is it commercial/sharing or with a local family)?
4   How far are you from where you will work?

5   Is it safe? For example, is the country at war? Are the streets safe after dark? Is it safe for a single man/woman? How volatile is the local political situation? Is there discrimination against certain ethnic groups? Is there a British embassy?

6   What about insurance: does your employer provide it and pay for it or do you have to? Does it cover repatriation if you become ill? Does it cover personal injury? Have you seen a copy of the policy to check the cover?

If you receive too many vague or unsatisfactory answers to these questions, think twice about going. Try to make enquiries about the company. Past students can be useful-ask the placement office for details. The university careers service might also have come across the organisation before.

Make sure that you get the employer to put everything in writing.

MISCELLANEOUS JOB-HUNTING SITES

'Outdoor' jobs can be found at Coolworks http://www.coolworks.com. See also:

www.workbank.man.ac.uk
www.barzone.co.uk
www.ex.ac.uk/jobsurfing
www.milkround.co.uk
www.topjobs.co.uk
www.jobsunlimited.co.uk
www.wcn.co.uk
www.stepstone.com
www.experienceworks.ncl.ac.uk

SELF-EMPLOYMENT

There is also a useful guide for students setting up businesses on the Liverpool John Moores web site at http://cwis.livjm.ac.uk/careers/sae/frames.htm.

If the business is e-commerce related, Yahoo! provides a guide to setting up a business on-line at http://smallbusiness.yahoo.com/. There is also help at http://www.virginbiz.net, which also gives a complete start-up guide and invites applications from would-be entrepreneurs.

HSBC bank has a good web site on business planning and has a software package that will help you to produce a full business plan and accounts at www.ukbusiness.hsbc.com/hsbc/sab.

See also Stutely, R. (2002) *The Definitive Business Plan: The Fast-track to Intelligent Business Planning for Executives and Entrepreneurs*, 2nd edn, published by the Financial Times.

For information on setting up a small business, try www.businesslink. gov.uk.

Case study: self-employment

The actual idea of starting my own business for my placement year was generated by a belief that I would gain more of an idea of how to manage a business and the situations that arise if I actually ran my own business, rather than if I took a more traditional placement.

Around Easter time my friend suggested we go together in an online partnership. The business would sell high-end fashion clothes e.g. Armani, Versace etc. This idea came about from our own interest in these types of clothes.

So we began from there. We contacted the business links first to put us in touch with suppliers and other people who would benefit the business.

I asked advice about the programming that I would need to know, how to get the web site published and other things I didn't previously know.

Once I knew what I needed I set about acting upon it.

We obtained books on HTML and basically taught ourselves. We learnt how to add graphics and pictures, how to animate objects and lots of other things, some of which we use on the site, others we don't.

The process of learning these skills is continual but it took us about a week to develop our first web site, but then a further two months to construct a site we were happy to publish – which looking back, was poor.

Then we went about advertising our site through *Loaded* magazine and online shopping malls and auctions. We were managing about 30 hits a day. It wasn't until Christmas that we made our first sale through the site.

However, since then we have been doing quite well with around 150 hits a day at present. Our store size has trebled and although it is quite a small operation, we are looking to introduce a shopping basket in the very near future, a process that should increase sales further.

Our ability to write HTML code also allowed us to design a web site for another business, and there is now another business that would like us to write a site for them.

So, all in all, I believe that I have learned many skills that I would not have learned if I had taken up a traditional placement year.

WEB RESOURCES

Excellent advice on a range of placement issues can be found at the National Council for Work Experience's web site at www.work-experience.org. This also lists many current vacancies.

Information booklets are also available from the Association of Graduate Careers Advisory Services (AGCAS) www.agcas.org.uk/ and www.agcasscotland.org.uk:

- going for interviews
- making applications
- mature or students
- the way forward

AGCAS also produce a useful video, 'Can I have a few minutes of your time?'

You could look at the Careers Services Unit (CSU), site http://www.prospects.CSU.ac.uk. This body publishers a number of leaflets and the other resources for students including;

- prospects directory
- prospects today
- prospects where?

USEFUL BOOKS

Interviews

Excel at Interviews, by Patricia McBride (1999) Lifetime Careers (Wiltshire) Ltd
Includes a section on college interviews as well as ways to practise with other people.
New edition May 2004.

Passing that Interview: How to Make Yourself the Winning Candidate, Judith Johnston (1997) How to Books
Takes you step-by-step through the essential pre-interview groundwork, the interview encounter itself and what you can learn from the experience afterwards.

Great Answers to Tough Interview Questions, Martin John Yate (2001) 5th edn, Kogan Page
Includes standard interview questions as well as more specific ones, with examples of how to answer and what you shouldn't say!

First Interviews – Sorted!, Chris Phillips (2002) GTI Specialist Publishers Ltd
A handbook on how to handle your first interview. Ideal reading if you
don't have much time to prepare!

Tackling Tough Interview Questions in a Week, Mo Shapiro and Alison
Straw (2002) Stoughton & Hodder

Welcome to the Real World: Make an Impression at Your Job Interview
by Gil Shidlo (1998) Interview Power.

Tests

How to Pass Graduate Recruitment Tests, Mike Bryon (1994) Kogan Page
Includes psychometric tests. Gives advice on how to prepare as well as
examples and practice tests.

How to Master Psychometric Tests, Mark Parkinson (2000) Kogan Page
Includes information on the tests, how to prepare for them and practice
questions.

How to Pass Computer Selection Tests, Sanjay Modha (1994) Kogan Page
Aimed at people taking selection tests in the computing field. Shows you
how the tests are organised, common mistakes, how to prepare and sample questions.

How to Pass Verbal Reasoning Tests, Harry Tolley and Ken Thomas
(1996) Kogan Page

How to Pass Numeracy Tests by Harry Tolley and Ken Thomas (2000)
Kogan Page

Understanding Psychometric Testing in a Week, Gareth Lewis and Gene
Crozier (1999) Hodder & Stoughton.

Presentations

Successful Presentation Skills, Andrew Bradbury (2000) 2nd edn. Kogan
Page
Includes tips on how to overcome nerves, be concise, understand body
language and use visual aids effectively. Also, how to be an effective communicator, structuring your presentation, making an impact and maintaining interest. This book is aimed at people in employment but makes
an ideal reference if you are planning a presentation for an interview.

Knockout Presentations: How to Deliver Your Message With Power, Punch &
Pizzazz, Diane DiResta (1998) Chandler House Press.

Assessment centres

How to Succeed at a Assessment Centres, Harry Tolley and Bob Wood (2001) Kogan Page
Covers the reasons for assessment centres, what skills and characteristics the assessors are looking for, what the main types of tests are and what the dos and don'ts are. Assessment Centres are used by many organisations and you might well be asked to attend an assessment day, in which case this is a really useful guide.

Once you've got the job!

Flying Start, Jo Gardiner (1999) Spiro Press
A guide to your first job and how to make a success of it. Including communications and interpersonal skills, time management, ways of working, problem areas – stress, handling difficult situations, and moving on from the job. There is also a section on employment law.

Beyond the CV: Securing a Lifetime of Work, Helen Vandeveld (1997) Butterworth-Heinemann
Gives advice on how to plan your career strategy. Shows you how to manage your career path, create your digital portfolio, develop on-line job searching skills, devise new career investment strategies and extend your creative horizons.

FINALLY, A WORD ABOUT HEALTH AND SAFETY

Whilst health and safety is something that we all expect to be able to take for granted you need to be aware of this when looking for a placement and when actually working. There is a range of legislation covering working premises and processes which started with the Health And Safety At Work Act in 1974.

Essentially the original and subsequent directives are based upon a general concept of a general duty of care for most people associated with work activities. The specific aims are to:

- secure the health, safety and welfare of persons at work
- protect persons other than persons at work against risks to health or safety arising out of, or in connection with, the activities of persons at work
- control the keeping and use of explosive or highly flammable or otherwise dangerous substances, and generally prevent the unlawful acquisition, possession and use of such substances

▨ control the emission into the atmosphere of noxious or offensive substances

It surprises many people that all parties in the employment relationship have a duty of care. Workers are responsible for their own and others' safety; it is not just the employer who needs to take the initiative. If there is something that you are not happy with or think might pose a risk to yourself or others you need to ensure that your concerns are known and that action is taken.

You should not have to work in a dangerous situation and ideally you should ensure in advance that the organisation takes health and safety seriously and that your work place is safe. Universities are also included in this duty of care when students are on placement and you will probably have to get your new employer to fill in a form confirming that appropriate policies are in place. However, if you choose to negotiate your own placement by taking a year off studies, then you will need to make your own checks.

The essence of health and safety is best summarised by an extract from the web site of the Health & Safety Executive.

So, what's health and safety all about?

In a nutshell, it's about preventing injuries and harm to health caused by work and that applies to employees, the self-employed and the public. It is also about providing a satisfactory workplace. Health and safety law applies to all work activities and to just about everyone, no matter how small the firm.

Employers are responsible for protecting people, not just their employees, from harm caused by work.

Employees have to take care of themselves and of others.

Suppliers of chemicals, machinery and equipment have to make sure their products or imports are safe, and provide information.

Contractors, designers, gas installers and those who transport dangerous goods also have responsibilities.

For full explanation and provisions see www.hse.gov.uk/aboutus/hsc/index.htm.

Appendix 1: example of skills audit

Based on a computing degree student with summer job in landscape gardening.

Skills/attributes	Examples
Business management skills	Not much so far. Present course contains two modules, introductions to management & finance. Observed two different bosses in summer job, both had different styles – learnt quite a bit.
Named specialist skills *(a catch-all term)*	Working competence in languages C++, FORTRAN, XML, COBOL.
Information technology *(can you use it easily?)*	No contest!
Cognitive skills *(thinking)*	Good at chess and strategy-based computer games. The final year of my degree is going to develop critical thinking skills.
Learning to learn *(can you learn fast and continue developing yourself?)*	Learnt many other computer skills on my own such as writing highly interactive websites (see own site at www . . .)
Communication skills	In landscape gardening although I was employed as a labourer all the planning was done on computer so I often got the job of using the laptop on site and then checking things we didn't understand with the designers.

Appendix 1 – *continued*	
Skills/attributes	*Examples*
Interpersonal skills/attributes	Getting on with the rest of the gardening team. I was the junior out of 12 guys and I had to learn how to get on with them and stand up for myself.
Unspecified high level skills *(analysis, synthesis, evaluation)*	This is one of the main skill sets of my degree. Looking at a problem, breaking it down into a series of tiny steps and then figuring out the best way of programming it so that to the end user it looks like a seamless solution.
Flexibility	I'd say adaptable rather than flexible. I don't mind having a go at anything.
Personal skills/attributes	My main quality is seeing a job through to the end and being able to persuade people in group situations. On hall social committee and one of two main organisers of the May Ball this coming year.
Practical/vocational skills/ qualifications *(experience)*	I suppose computing is my main vocational skill – I don't think I'd make a living as a gardener.
Foreign languages	GCSE French (just!)
Unspecified 'key' or 'core' skills *(transferable skills)*	Good at writing reports but not essays where I get lost without a clear structure to follow.
Numerical skills	OK at maths but don't get much practice at arithmetic.
Other	

Comment

Note how the student has brought a wide range of work, academic and personal situations into the analysis. There are some gaps, of course; let's call them development opportunities. There is a strong sense that this student is looking forwards to his final year as well as backwards into past experiences.

Appendix 2: questions to ask admission tutors and programme leaders

Does the programme include a placement? Is this mandatory or optional? How long is the minimum placement period?

Note that while an optional placement sounds attractive in the sense that it will obviously keep your options open you must be prepared to leave behind many of the friends that you have made in the first year when you go out on placement. This can in practice deter many students from actually taking up a placement.

With an optional placement you should ask what percentage of students on a particular programme go out on placement.

Whose responsibility is it to find a suitable position?
What help and support is available from university for job searching?

This may take the form of merely providing information to students, possibly through a careers centre, or alternatively it could involve specialist preparation sessions and the guidance of a personal tutor. Ask if employer career fairs are held on campus. Many universities have employers that take students year after year, often interviewing students on site; this will significantly cut down travelling when you need to be getting on with your studies in the second year.

It may be the case, and this is more unusual these days, that it is the university that will decide which employer you will go to, and perhaps which line of work/task is most suited to you.

What proportion of those seeking placement are successful?
Is the placement experience recognised?

For example, is there a separate certificate or diploma to evidence the work experience gained and assessments made?

Does the placement count towards the degree classification?
Does the placement have to be completed satisfactorily to allow progression to the final year of study?

Note that if the answer to either of the two questions above is yes, then you should ask how it is to be assessed.

Are students visited out on placement? And if so, how often?
Do you think that by doing a placement in this particular subject will improve my employment prospects after graduation/qualification?
What are typical salaries on placement?

You might also enquire about living expenses if placements tend to be offered in an expensive part of the country/world.

Does the institutions follow the QAA and NCWE codes of practice for placement?

Appendix 3: the benefits of employing placement students

The following might be useful when trying for a job with an employer that hasn't employed a placement student before and for inspiration before writing letters of application and preparing for interviews. Young people have a great deal to offer employers, especially during a placement; don't undersell yourself!

Employers quote the following reasons for employing students:

- well-motivated employees able to combine youthful energy, enthusiasm and fresh insights with theoretical knowledge
- a means of securing a valuable human resource, particularly when operational flexibility is required
- recruitment without advertising or agency fees
- the opportunity to assess students during an 'extended interview' as potential employees in the future
- up to date knowledge: our students are conversant with areas such as Information Technology, Accounts, Business Law, Languages, Marketing, Research and Personnel Management
- the satisfaction of playing an important role in providing tomorrow's managers with the experience they need today
- the opportunity to raise your company's profile with business graduates

WHAT SKILLS DO STUDENTS HAVE?

The following list shows the broad range of transferable skills and qualities that might be found in students studying business degrees. Think about other skills that are relevant to your own subject area.

1   *People skills*: communication, listening, persuasion, discretion, effective group participation, team work, self-development, time management.
2   *Management skills*: team management, leadership, creativity, planning, project management.
3   *Business analysis skills*: statistical applications, problem-solving, decision-making, management of change.
4   *Business practice skills*: numeracy, organisational ability, memo and report writing, telephone manner, keyboard skills.
5   *Information technology skills*: application of IT to the business environment, hardware and software selection, text handling, data analysis, information retrieval.
6   *Marketing Skills*: selling, presentations, public relations, market research and analysis, consumer behaviour.
7   *Accounting skills*: understanding accounting concepts, conventions and ratios, interpreting financial information, evaluating costs, IT applications, budget statements, reviewing published accounts.
8   *Legal and economic skills*: law as a regulatory factor in business, identifying and resolving legal problems, European Community Law, awareness of international and multi-national aspects of business.
9   *European language skills*: oral, reading and writing skills in specified languages, awareness of the cultural and business environment of EU countries.
10 *Tourism skills*: customer friendly, consumer friendly, employee friendly as well as the above management, people and business skills.

Source: Derbyshire Business School marketing literature.

Appendix 4: example of placement experience record (1)

3.0 Student's Role and Contribution to the Organisation

My position is held in the Club Promotions division of the Promotions department. The other divisions of the promotions department are TV and Radio Promotions. The fundamental aim of what is known as XYZ:Club is to promote artists at club and specialist radio level and to form relationships with the clubs, stations and their DJs. This is achieved by supplying DJs nation-wide with XYZ's music in order that it is heard by the music buying public in clubs and on specialist radio. The onus is to create a 'buzz' around XYZ's records with the obvious aim being to stimulate sales. Thus relationships with DJs, specialist radio and specialist shops are constantly maintained and improved.

As a placement student the title of the position I hold is Club Promotions Assistant. The key purpose of my role is to promote XYZ records and artists at club level as well as at specialist radio, press and retail levels. I also provide assistance to the Head of Club Promotions, the Dance Promotions Co-ordinator and the Urban Promotions Co-ordinator in the running of the department.

3.1 Key Responsibilities

- Assistance in co-ordinating XYZ's dance database held by Club Promotions;
- Liase with club and specialist radio DJs, specialist press and specialist shops in order to assess record and artist potential and ensure exposure at front-line level;

229

- Assist in liaison with all XYZ departments where club promotions activity is deemed necessary;
- Contribution to weekly report on relevant dance acts;
- Compiling and formulating DJ reaction sheets for new records;
- Compiling DJ's playlists and weekly chart returns;
- Participation in travel to relevant club nights, festivals, music concerts, specialist radio and retail activities (including in-store signings) across the U.K. in order to promote music and artists;
- Research and understand competitor's dance promotions strategies;
- Organise mass 'on-line' mailouts.

The execution of the outlined responsibilities results in the profile of XYZ's products being raised. The promotional activity at the specialist levels also provides useful feedback in terms of the potential of a new release. For example the DJ reactions that I formulate on the database will create an overall consensus on a particular record. The comments the DJs make regarding the way in which the general public reacts to a record when played provides extremely important marketing information for the company. The process of mass 'on-line' mail-outs to DJ's e-mail addresses regarding forthcoming tracks and re-mixes also adds to the 'buzz' that we aim to develop.

4.0 Analysis of Skills and Competencies Enhanced

There were a number of skills and attributes that were required in order to gain my placement position. These are outlined below:

- Organisational/planning abilities;
- Self motivation/drive;
- Ability to work under pressure;
- Creativity;
- Initiative;
- High level of stamina;
- Outgoing personality;
- Independent minded;
- Possess maturity to handle a stand alone role;
- Word processing, spreadsheet, e-mail and Internet skills.

However the work that I have undertaken during the initial 6 months of my placement has enabled me to improve a number of these skills. I feel I have also acquired additional attributes during this period. These advancements in my transferable skills are outlined in the following sections.

4.1 Interpersonal Skills

My role as Club Promotions Assistant has required me to communicate with a range of people in a number of different formats. I have learnt how to relate to my colleagues as well as how to liase with business contacts and customers. I have developed my writing skills by contributing to the weekly report on the dance acts, writing internal memos and writing letters and e-mails to DJs on the database. My listening and verbal skills have also been advanced. For example I endeavour to create a positive image for a particular record (product) when I speak to a DJ/journalist.

4.2 Working and Relating to Others

This is an area in which I feel I have significantly benefited as a result of my placement. I constantly have to interact with members of the department as well as with the DJs we service and the general public. This has led to a growth in confidence. I feel I am now more assertive and can negotiate when necessary. For example, a particular requirement of my job is to screen the DJs who aspire to be on our database and receive free music. I firstly check the amount of people they play to each week and make sure they are returning their charts and play-lists to all the relevant dance press.

The next step is to ultimately decide whether it is beneficial for XYZ to use them to promote new music.

4.3 Personal Skills

The fact that a major part of my role within Club Promotions is to assist all the other members of the department has meant I must manage my time efficiently. For example I may be working on a promotional project for the Dance Promotions Co-ordinator when I will be called upon to help with a project being undertaken by the Urban Promotions Co-ordinator. Thus I must meet deadlines and be flexible.

Another 'personal skill' I have developed is the ability to cope with stress. There are often instances when deadlines must be met. This is particularly true when organising a mail-out of a new record to the DJs on the mailing list. It is my responsibility to ensure the records are sent out in time to be received by the DJs before the weekend in order that they can place them in their individual play-lists and charts for publication the following week.

4.4 Self-Development

I believe the experience I have gained in my role has led to an improvement in my creativity. For example I am often asked to write the 'blurb' for the music we are promoting. This involves detailing an artist's history and the current record's musical strengths. This 'blurb' sheet acts as a useful tool in providing DJs, specialist radio and press with information with which to promote our products. Other areas I have developed include the ability to solve problems when they arise and to be able to learn from my mistakes.

4.5 Knowledge

There have been particular instances when I have applied theory from my first and second year marketing studies. A prime example of this has been the organisation of focus groups. These have been conducted in order to gain primary research information. I arrange for 'club-goers' to come to the office and listen to a number of potential releases. The information they provide is extremely useful in deciding which records will stimulate the most sales. Also the use of a database as a promotional/marketing tool is an area I have previously covered. I am constantly trying to add to this database and it is central to the operation of the department. I will continue to try to apply as much of my subject knowledge to my placement whenever I can.

4.6 Information Technology (IT)

The role of Club Promotions Assistant requires me to be proficient in terms of PC skills. I have improved my word processing skills through writing letters, creating 'blurb' sheets and contributing to reports. I am responsible for the maintenance of the department's database and my email skills have been enhanced due to the constant use of e-mail to communicate with staff members and clients/contacts. The Internet is also constantly cited as a source of information regarding competitor products. In addition to this, specific XYZ applications have also been used e.g. placing purchase orders.

5.0 Personal Development Programme

Although I have made notable improvements to my transferable skills it is imperative that I strive to continue these advancements in order to maximise the effectiveness of my placement. In order to do this the programme below has been devised in agreement with my supervisor, the Head of Club Promotions. The programme is comprised of a number of objectives and tasks to be fulfilled in the coming months up until the conclusion of my placement:

- Additional involvement with promotional strategy. Including attending more meetings and having a degree of input into this field. Thus applying more theory from my subject area.
- Have sole responsibility in forming the weekly Club Promotions report. The key aim of this is to further my report writing skills. This will also involve elements of market research of both primary and secondary nature.
- Undertake a specialist project that will result in a presentation. This will include the use of visual and audio aids as well as the handling of questions. Jamie and myself will set a topic that needs investigating and I will present the findings to the relevant departments.
- Visit the mastering/cutting house in order to see the development of the product/music. This will be followed by spending time with the Creative Department to see the creation of the artwork for sleeves etc.

This should provide me with a better understanding of the stages of product development.

- Spend time in other departments in the company. The areas covered will be Sales, New Media, Artist and Repertoire, Press and Creative Services.
- Visit specialist retailers in order to cement relationships. This will aim to enhance communication skills and overall confidence.
- Develop PC skills through the use of more software packages. E.g. Power-Point and Excel.

Appendix 5: example of placement experience record (2)

Role

Key Tasks:

- Marketing Analysis and Competitor information gathering
- Product inspection and information gathering to meet with ISO 9002 requirements
- Assisting Product Managers with new product development and other related tasks as necessary
- Imperial (sister brand) sales forecasting and ordering
- Day-to-day assistance to the Product Manager

(*Source*: Placement Student Job Description)

At the start of my placement I had a 10-week hand over period with the previous placement student which allowed me to see the possibilities my role had in the coming 14 months while I trained towards that role. In retrospect I feel the expectations I had with regard to promotional [in marketing terms not advancement] experience have not been met, but this is covered later in the report.

My first responsible role was to create and update a spreadsheet tracking low stock to make sure that late orders came through on time. This was my first involvement in liasing with company employees in Germany and suppliers in France and Italy. The Procurement department is now using my spreadsheet when a member of staff was employed to take on this task full time.

At the beginning of every month, I compile figures on the previous month's company performance (domestic appliances) for use in the monthly sales meeting. This information includes sales, value, costs and profit performance, all of which must be put into a presentation for the meeting. I am also involved in compiling presentations of a product nature for the Sales meeting.

One of the most enjoyable projects I have been involved in recently is a competitor and Market analysis with a view to extending the food preparation range. There were two aspects to this research.

Firstly as I am the main liaison with our Market Research agency, I contacted them for recent market information on the food preparation sector. Using this I was able to analyse trends occurring in the market, an obvious example of which would be a trend toward stainless steel appliances in the kitchen.

The second aspect of this project involved a competitor analysis, the main objective of which is to see if some competition are catching on to trends earlier than others and to make sure that we don't miss taking advantage of a trend.

Skills Acquired and Enhanced

Seven months into my placement I have had a regular and in depth use of Word, Excel, PowerPoint, Lotus Notes and SAP (stock and sales tracking database).

My understanding of marketing processes such as pricing and promotional strategies as well as the importance of PR has been enhanced through regular involvement in product range meetings and informal discussions.

I have enhanced my ability to handle customer enquiries and complaints through regular contact with customers over the phone. Also I have had the opportunity to go on several visits to retailers where I have met both retailers and customers and listened, first hand to their views on the products and services we offer.

Further Development Plans

Working for the product department I have had some invaluable experience with regards to the pricing and product aspects of marketing. However I intend to organise to spend some time with Marketing Services to enhance the promotional side of my role. I will help to organise point of sale material for a new product range in the department stores, and hopefully have some input into the layout of our new brochures. Further to that, I believe time spent with our creative consultancy would be an interesting experience to follow the processes involved in making a television commercial.

Time management is an area that caused me most difficulty and I have found that workloads can fluctuate quite significantly. To overcome this I have started keeping a comprehensive diary and I have found this has helped me in meeting deadlines.

At the start of my placement with XYZ I was placed on a three-day intensive training course to rapidly improve my product knowledge. The course has been designed to train retailers in the benefits of company products. This enabled me to assist managers and deal with any problem enquiries regarding our products. However I am frequently asked about issues of a technical nature that are beyond my knowledge and I therefore plan to attend a technical training course next month.

Glossary

Assessment	Monitoring and critical evaluation by an academic, in conjunction with the employer's representative, of a student work experience against agreed criteria and standards. Assessment does not necessarily lead to accreditation.
Internships	A phrase common in the United States that is increasingly used by large companies in the UK. and refers to a placement within their organisation.
Key skills	Specific attributes and attitudes sought by potential employers. They may include specialist technical skills but more generally they include the transferable skills. The Qualifications and Curriculum Authority has identified six key skills: communication, application of number, information technology, working with others, improving learning and performance, and problem-solving.
Mentor	A person who is usually had an employee other has companies who will be assigned to guide the student throughout the course of the placement. They may not work directly with the student but are a point of contact for advice and help throughout the placement.
Part-time work	Paid or unpaid work undertaken during term-time. For a project that is providing assessment and accreditation of part-time work look at the Careers Research and Advisor Centre Insight Plus programme on www.insightplus.co.uk.
Specialist skills	Specialist skills are those relating to the subject matter and techniques of the degree programme or of the academic discipline.
Transferable skills	Are skills that are gained while working or learning that can be applied quickly productively to another situation.
Voluntary work	Any type of work undertaken for no or nominal remuneration, usually outside an academic institution. It is usually but not always taken to denote charitable

	or community-based work. It may be part-time or full-time.
Work-based project	A specific piece of assessed work for a course, undertaken at an employer's premises.
Work placements	A period of paid or unpaid work that is usually undertaken as part of the programme of study. It may be arranged by the institute of higher education through which study is taking place, or in conjunction with the employer. Alternatively, the student may arrange it directly with the employer. Placements are generally assessed and this assessment may be accredited as part of the degree course.
Workplace learning	Is that learning which takes place directly from being employed.
Work shadowing	Where a student observes a member of staff working in an organisation. It is usually short term and is appropriate where a detailed knowledge of a particular task is not required or where it is not possible for a student to actually undertake a particular task (for example, in conducting negotiations with the customer or handling dangerous chemicals, etc.).

Index